THE GARDEN REBORN

Bringing New Life To Your Aging Landscape

Ruby Weinberg

Photographs by Martin Weinberg

Green Valley Press

Library of Congress Card Number 2004108500

ISBN 0-9758878-0-7

Publisher's Cataloging-in-Publication
(Provided by Quality Books Inc.)

Weinberg, Ruby.
   The garden reborn : bringing new life to your aging
landscape / by Ruby Weinberg ; photographs, Martin
Weinberg.
   p. cm.
   Includes index.
   LCCN 2004108500
   ISBN 0-97588780-7

   1. Landscape gardening.   I. Title.
   SB473.W45 2004   712'.6
   QBI04-200295

Green Valley Press
P.O. Box 542
Califon, NJ 07830-3434
Phone 908-832-6609
Fax 908-832-6609
e-mail: greenvalleypress@earthlink.net

Printed in the U.S.A.
Stuyvesant Press Inc
Irvington, N.J.

DEDICATION

To My Husband, Martin
Mere words cannot express the depths of my love and appreciation for this most remarkable
of human beings

TABLE OF CONTENTS

Chapter IX. PERPLEXING PERENNIALS
Definition of "herbaceous perennials"
The difference between borders, beds, and island beds
Weed control in perennial areas
The pros and cons of zonal listings
Elimination of those perennials that require high maintenance

Chapter X. AWAY WITH THE FUSSY, ON WITH THE ENDURING
Renovating the time-consuming perennial border
Addition of perennials with dark foliage colors
Selection of newly introduced cultivars for special effects
Treatment of shady areas with attractive perennials
How to determine perennials that are reliable in your area
Perennials for the Mid-Atlantic states with proven longevity

Chapter XI. LOVE THAT LAWN
The private home lawn—an American dream come true
Brief history of lawn culture
The necessity of an adequate water supply and rainfall for growing any lawn
Whether to restore vitality to an old lawn or to start afresh with a new lawn
Discussion of cultural needs for a low maintenance lawn
The addition of slow release fertilizers and organic matter
Labor saving equipment for ease in lawn maintenance

Chapter XII. TO KEEP OR GRUB THAT FLOWERING SHRUB
Evaluation of the condition of aging shrubs
Adding new shrubs that are the first of the season to bloom
Adding shrubs that bloom during the summer gap
Discussion of native vs. introduced shrubs
Eradicating shrubs with run-away tendencies
Special shrubs for special effects
Adding shrubs that attract bird populations
Case history of a shrub removal project
Pruning flowering shrubs

PREFACE

In this book, I share with you some of my dilemmas, mistakes, ideas, convictions, and triumphs in the field of landscape gardening. It is a calling that has occupied much of my time and energy for over forty-five years, both as a professional designer and as a hobby gardener. In more recent years, the hobby part has quite overtaken the business end of my activities as three or four cultivated acres (out of six) at Frog Pond Farm have become more interesting. As you will read, the initial landscaping of this garden was quite a challenge for my husband and me. More than three decades later, several parts of our garden once again needed serious attention.

A few years ago, I came to the full realization that "the bird of time has but a little way to fly—and Lo! The bird is on the wing." None of us, of course, can be sure how long we will live, but while this gardener and her mate still have our health, we intend to continue repairing those aging parts of our garden that need to be refreshed. We began these renovation projects along with our usual maintenance chores. But these days, working at a slower pace than formerly, the occasional help of a strong, young assistant speeds each project along.

In the past, whenever I had been called upon to plan landscaping around a new house on an undeveloped property, a rush of exciting possibilities filled my head. Yet, when working on an older site, especially one that had been landscaped by do-it-yourself gardeners, many decisions always seemed painful to both client and designer. Why? Because we are all loathe to undo even a small part of a garden that initially required a great deal of work. It's like pulling teeth to convince someone to chop down a sick tree that he or she had planted but no longer serves any purpose. Often, gardeners find it hard to believe that not every tree species will grow into a handsome Methuselah! But times change, our needs change and older plants sometimes pass their prime or overgrow their sites. Then too, the hardscaping may not have held up well with the passing of many years. Perhaps even more importantly, our taste also changes. Conversely, as we grow older and our physical strength weakens, our aesthetic ideas usually become more sophisticated!

Home ownership is a blessing to be treated with pride and care. For many, a major part of its joy is beautiful landscaping. A satisfying renovation will not only suit your own personal requisites, but also gives pleasure to your friends, family, and garden loving visitors.

In monetary terms, never a factor to be lightly dismissed, attractive landscaping should increase the value of your home by at least 15%.

Think of The Garden Reborn as the flame to ignite the candle with which to light your early attempts at garden renovation. Because home landscaping involves such a variety of elements, some of what you will read here is in detail while other parts might seem sketchy.

For example, if you are planning on building a small section of a low dry-laid rock wall, then my description of the work involved may be perfectly adequate to your needs. However, if this will be an extensive project with a long stretch of wall or walls that are over 3' in height, then you will need to research the topic quite thoroughly. (See Recommended Reading). After learning exactly what is involved, you might be encouraged to say "Yes, I believe that this job is well within my capabilities." Or, perhaps, if it demands the kind of machinery that you do not have, reality will set in and you'll decide that this is really an undertaking that requires the experience and equipment of a professional.

The Garden Reborn's prime purpose is to help you develop a plan of action for renovating your outdoor areas It is older landscaping that is discussed here for nature is not always kind to aging man nor to his aging garden. Given a choice, however, few gardeners would exchange their mature specimens for the newly planted. Rejoice at what already exists that more than meets with your approval, but revitalize the rest by embarking on some of the suggested projects within these pages. The written word cannot perform the labor of a renovation, but hopefully, the information within will ease and guide your work as you transform your property into a very special paradise.

CHAPTER I

WILDERNESS IS PARADISE?

CHAPTER I
Wilderness Is Paradise?

There comes a time in the life of an older garden when the addition of a few more pots of petunias will make little difference. In a sober moment of critical judgment, you, the homeowner, realize that your garden is aging and in places, not so gracefully. Little fixes will not be noticed because they may be overshadowed by a series of larger problems. In the thirtieth year of its existence, our own garden needed some major and minor repairs, and we set about accomplishing them.

Every garden shows its age in its own inimitable way. Perhaps yours is becoming engulfed in shrubbery. Or maybe you are faced with far too many dull and shady areas. Or possibly, your taste has changed. Once, you cherished a few garden ornaments such as that concrete dolphin that has stood for years near your swimming pool. Now, it looks to you like nothing more than a fish out of water. Removing such an ornament is easy, but facing up to the necessary big fixes is quite another matter. You know that it is going to require your time, attention, and money.

There is a good deal of charm and warmth in a home that you have occupied for many long years, or possibly, that several generations before you have occupied. Yet, despite the tender, loving care you may have lavished on your garden, the passing of more than twenty years brings about an inevitable transformation. In places, Mother Nature may now be in control, and not you, the caretaker of this property.

Unless a natural disaster has swept away your work, this is no time to mourn the toll taken by the passing years. It is a time, rather, to celebrate the marvels of maturity. What a wonder it is that your sapling trees and mail order shrubs, so fragile when first planted, have now grown into splendid specimens. Those small perennials that were planted bare root and looked so insignificant when obtained are now fat and floriferous. Perhaps some of your hardscaping features—such as a well constructed deck—have stood the test of time in beautiful condition. Why then allow anything degraded, inconvenient, or unsafe to mar the whole?

Possibly you have only recently purchased this older home. After renovating the interior, you now walk around outdoors to get a better look. One of the things that might have drawn you to this place was its mature shade trees, billowing flowering shrubs, splendid conifers, or large clumps of perennials scattered here and there. If your first view of this garden was in spring, then it is easy to understand why you determined to own the property. Is there any sight more compelling than fully developed landscape plantings in May or June? "Well," you told yourself, recalling your former experiences, "this is one garden in which we will not have to start from scratch."

5

In the long, cool light that comes with reflection and close inspection, you begin to ac-knowledge that parts of your garden are overgrown, or in some places, barren and yielding of nothing but weeds. How, then, are you going to revitalize your garden so that it meets your present needs and desires? Where a great deal of garden activity has taken place, far too many ornamentals may have been planted or far too many that have overgrown their site. Your garden is beginning to look like a wilderness area. Wilderness, at first, may seem like paradise, but it is not an ideal place to entertain your friends, dine alfresco, and, if you have small children, watch them play in safety. If you wish, you can travel occasionally to observe raw nature in a wilderness area. It is quite another thing to maintain your own little paradise-under-control where you can enjoy beauty close at hand every day of the year.

Some time ago, the full extent of our own garden's growth hit me like a lead balloon, or more properly, a hot air balloon. I remember standing on the lawn of our small rear garden that day. About 50' from our house, and running parallel to it, is a small brook. A rather steep upward sloping hillside, backed by a woodland, rises above this brook. In our earliest days here, this area had been planted with small hemlocks, leucothoe, rhododendrons and azaleas, all spaced far enough apart for future growth. As I stood there that day, I heard the "psst, poof," from the propane heater of a helium balloon overhead. Above the treetops, I spotted the balloon and its four or five occupants. "Land on our field," I called up to them, and they proceeded to do so. The troupe of happy balloonists tumbled out of the basket, offered us some champagne, and then enjoyed a walk through our garden. "Ah, we have landed in Shangri-la," one of them said. Such a compliment is difficult to forget!

Ten years later, on this same spot, I heard another balloon behind the woodland and planted slope. It was then that I realized how tall and thick it had all become. Now, only for a brief moment, could I see the balloon. It floated away, its occupants unaware of my presence.

Like the changes in children, we do not always realize how quickly many plants grow, and how the garden that we love may develop in a way that does not completely suit us. In this case, our hillside had become a lovely privacy shield, but several other parts of our garden were not faring so well.

One look at our railroad tie retainer wall along the drive, thirty years after its installa-tion, revealed that it had become a rotting, sagging hulk badly in need of replacement. The half acre pond in front of our house, so cool, and clean that it had long supported rainbow trout, was now a weed and algae infested soup every midsummer. A grouping of blue hol-lies had grown taller than their original labels indicated and the conifers behind them had been smothered into unrecognizable forms. Straggly bittersweet vines clambered high into their branches. Deer damage was everywhere, especially in my rock garden where the ani-mals had not-so-nimbly stepped on my delicate plants. The outer edges of the garden were hit the worst as native trees were being destroyed not only by overpopulations of deer but by wild honeysuckles and multiflora roses. Thirty years after the property was first developed, my husband and I gradually set about making some changes concentrating first on the cultivated areas and leaving the verges for a future date.

These problems, of course, are not necessarily the same ones that are haunting you. Everything is on a rather overwhelming scale if you have a bit of acreage and you are a "do-it-yourself" gardener. Whatever your property's size, wherever you live, in a rural area, suburb, or in a city, you can expect that several decades after your initial landscaping, both major and minor changes will be necessary to sustain beauty and usefulness.

Making changes requires that you reflect on your current ideas of enchantment, convenience, and manageable maintenance. These days, our leisure time is being barraged with many recreational enticements. Even if you have always been an active gardener, you may now be planning to eliminate some of the time consuming chores that require more attention than you are willing to give.

We cannot blame all our gardening problems on Mother Nature. Remember that spiraling conifer that you plunked down a small fortune to purchase? Your partner may have discouraged you from buying it, but it looked so interesting that you had to have it. You planted it in one location, then dug it up and replanted it in another, but the little tree always looked dreadful. It did not fit in with the rest of your plantings! Finally, the conifer died on an unprecedented frigid winter day. In a way, its loss was a relief. Experienced gardeners learn from their mistakes. Select the site before selecting the plant!

As a young woman and a totally inexperienced gardener, I followed the lead of my neighbors and planted a Canadian hemlock *(Tsuga canadensis)* on each front corner of our small suburban house. In my shortsighted ignorance, I did not take into account the fact that these hemlocks, in nature, are forest trees that sometimes grow to a height of 100'. I watched as mine reached 10' in less than ten years, and as they headed toward the sky, I began an endless series of drastic prunings to keep them in check. This accomplished, I observed that they now looked as miserable as prisoners shackled in chains. The misuse of woodland trees is all too common everywhere in our home landscaping.

It is easy to understand how many older home properties have become overgrown. As recently as twenty-five years ago, the number of dwarf and slow growing ornamentals available to gardeners was decidedly limited, especially in the northeastern and mid-western states. As a landscape designer/contractor in those days, I found many nursery offerings to be uninspiring. Almost every home garden was planted with what nurseries call their bread-and butter stock, typical of which was the upright *Taxus capitata*, spreading *Juniperus chinensis* pfitzeriana, and winter rusty *Thuja occidentalis*. And oh yes, that ubiquitous blue Colorado spruce, *Picea pungens*. Many such plantings were even placed in or near the foundation where space to expand is usually limited. Particularly troubling were the many yews, Taxus media hybrids which are between the English and Japanese species and are still all too prevalent in the landscape. Great walls of yews, centuries old, are proud ornamentation in many historic British gardens but most of them were probably planted on great estates when labor was both cheap and plentiful. Eventually, most yews grow into green giants that must be sheared at least once or twice every year. In foundation plantings, this leads to the creation of globes and polygons, nothing like nature intended. If ever there was a time consuming and unrewarding job, pruning yews should be placed at the head of the list.

Imagine my delight when I found a nursery in my area that specialized in dwarf and slow growing ornamentals. It was, however, always a problem to convince my clients that some slow growing 10" conifer cultivars are worth every penny of their price when compared with 3' to 4' seedlings of unknown lineage.

If and when you select the right plant for the right place, heavy annual pruning should not be necessary. Experienced gardeners are learning to fully appreciate the lasting power of slow growers. Unless you have a broad space to fill (certainly not in most foundation plantings) fast growing conifers and shrubs usually have to be replaced sooner than we expect, sooner than we wish. With so many marvelous species available to us now, we can be highly selective about choosing those that remain a reasonable size for a very long time.

Now that you are renovating areas of your garden, you will want to consult trustworthy reference books to help determine the growth rates of individual plants. If you have moved to your present home from afar, it is also a good idea to meet with your county agricultural agent who can clue you in on how tall and broad a specific plant might grow in twenty or thirty years. Twenty years, you say? What now seems like a long time will speed by like a marathon runner when you've become a senior citizen. No garden will provide enjoyment if it becomes a place where too much is squeezed into too small a space.

Common Problems:

1. Some of your hardscaping needs repair. Paving materials such as concrete or asphalt have a tendency to buckle or crack after many years; railroad ties rot, trellises, arbors, benches, etc., may also show signs of the corrosive force of nature
2. The prized views from your window are now obscured by shrubbery.
3. Design errors, such as a path that is seldom used or leads to nowhere special, result in wasted spaces that could be utilized in a more effective manner.
4. Every gentle rainfall brings down a multitude of twigs and branches on your lawn.

Your trees are telling you something; they need heavy pruning!

5. Improperly pruned trees and shrubs have grown malformed and are now far more subject to entry of disease.

6. Where, oh where, have your flowers gone? Some are now engulfed in the shade of a canopy that shuts off so much light that few can flourish.

7. A vigorous lawn, without an edging strip, constantly creeps into every planting bed making the lawn, itself, difficult to mow.

8. Brambly plants too close to a path, like wayward children pulling at their mothers' skirts, scrape your legs with every passing.

9. So many unusual specimen plants dot your beds, borders, and lawn areas that you've created a restless atmosphere rather than the serene habitat that was your intention.

10. Some plants remain that are terribly susceptible to insect or disease damage.

11. Ornamentals that hate "wet feet" look dreadful or are slowly dying in places that are poorly drained.

12. Gentle slopes have now become steep and bare—or weed infested.

13. The winter scene in your garden is unattractive because far too many areas have been devoted to beds where flowering perennials are in their invisible, dormant stage.

14. Changes in your neighborhood, such as newly constructed homes nearby, have also changed your views, your soil drainage, and the volume of noise.

15. A few areas of your garden, demanding of summer irrigation, are too far from a convenient water source.

16. Half dead plants, despite your optimistic appraisal, have not been removed although they are well on their way to becoming food for worms.

These are but a few signs of the deterioration that you might encounter with the passing of time. Large or small, irritating or enormously displeasing, they can certainly interfere with the pleasure and maintenance of a garden. Your list of problems may be somewhat different, but now, having faced up to their existence, you are determined to revitalize as much of your garden as possible given your time, strength, and financial limitations.

Every morning, as we catch a glimpse of our own image in the mirror, we are well aware of the changes that time has wrought. Although we realize that some effort is necessary to preserve our strength, our health, and our good looks, we might be slow to admit that it also takes a substantial effort to revitalize our landscaping. Rather than feeling discouraged, if you have many areas that need work, always keep in mind the fact that each and every step you take will immediately bring the garden that you love that much closer to your overall perception of beauty.

Where to begin? The secret to successful renovation is to plan first and then work at a slow but steady pace giving yourself one or many years to get the job done. If you have been a do-everything-yourself gardener but are no longer young and strong, realize that some projects, for your own safety, will require a hired helping hand. Or, if you feel overwhelmed by a series of complex problems requiring complex solutions, then what you might need most is the advice of a professional landscape designer or architect. When a satisfactory plan of attack has been initiated, it is amazing how well an experienced do-it-yourself gardener can follow through on the project at hand.

Just think—when it is all accomplished how proud you will be to be able to proclaim "Our garden has been reborn."

CHAPTER II
NEW VIEWS FROM OLD WINDOWS

CHAPTER II
New Views From Old Windows

In the greater part of the United States, most of us spend four or five months looking out at our gardens rather than walking through them. If we neglect to fully develop exciting scenes from the windows of our homes, we are missing something. The more severe the climate, the more important is this usually forgotten aspect of landscape design. Like improving our personal appearance, landscape revitalization should begin from within. Clear, uncluttered windows with interesting views bring us into the garden every month of the year, regardless of the weather. If you work at home, then you can appreciate how great this is. If you work outside the home, you will all the more crave a look into your garden when you return or on weekends when it's too cold, rainy, or snowy to venture outdoors. For the handicapped or the temporarily ill, a view garden can make the difference between optimism and depression.

Some years ago, my husband and I were standing on a path overlooking a lake in England. The place that we were visiting was Stourhead, the celebrated eighteenth century romantic garden. The bridge that crossed the lake was reflected in the water, its graceful arches appearing as great, misty ovals. "What a grand vista," I remarked. "Why do you say grand?" replied my husband. "Aren't all vistas grand?" I thought about that. The word vista implies, if not means, something glorious with plenty of space between the viewer and what he views. Can you imagine describing a utility such as a water tower on the horizon as a vista? My husband was right in that all true vistas are grand.

There are, of course, many gardens that borrow for their background the ocean, the mountains, great expanses of meadows, or other spectacular scenery. However, for most of us, our views are far more modest and perhaps uninviting. When this is the case, we can all create attractive outdoor scenes within our gardens by drawing the viewer's attention to the near rather than the far. Using the windows of our homes, what we will see is a picture within a frame.

Even if professionals originally landscaped your garden, view gardens may not have been part of their design. Landscape contractors, including those with artistic ability, are first and foremost outdoorsmen. They might have overlooked the fact that the homeowner may not have the time and energy to get out into their gardens during all the seasons.

This aspect, pleasing garden views, was so important to us that my husband and I decided to seek them out--or create them in a likely area--when we moved to our rural property from the suburbs. We purchased a six acre plot in a valley surrounded by heavily forested low hills. A small, poorly drained field backed by wet woodland occupied half the site. A farmer had used the field for grazing cows—but only in an emergency. A water filled gully separated the field from the second section where an unsightly swamp filled the lower area. A tangle of alders and brambles choked the murky water and was certainly not a view that we wanted to live with. Offsetting this "problem" was the gully itself. Here, fresh, clear spring waters flowed every month of the year, according to neighbors. It eventually reaches Frog Hollow Brook at the foot of the hill. Recognizing that water of this quality is a most precious resource, it was obvious to us that here was a perfect pond site! Our view garden of the future was now beginning to reveal itself.

On the slope above the swamp is a lightly wooded knoll. A giant white oak tree borders the knoll indicating that the drainage patterns here were under control. This, we knew, was a perfect house site.

Yet, it was easy to understand why many a prospective buyer before us had rejected the property. It was wild and wet and required a great deal of work to transform the whole into a pleasing pastoral scene. Ah, the innocence and ambition of youth!

A full six months before house construction, my husband, with the help of a friend, cleared the site with a brush cutter, and then called in a state soil conservation agent to help us engineer a half acre pond to replace the swamp. The runaway spring waters from the gully were temporarily diverted. Next, a huge bulldozer dug the pond 65' from the house site. It was frightening when we looked into that deep, empty hole, but the gully waters soon returned to their original path and filled that ugly cavity in only a matter of weeks. It had become a body of pure spring water. As for the gully—a footbridge was built across it. Landscaping on both banks transformed it into an attractive "babbling brook."

One thing was for certain; every croaking frog for miles around seemed happy to have settled on or near the water. Songbirds also were happy to have a place to swoop and dip their beaks, and waterfowl began to gather here finding the pond a perfect little sanctuary. The bass and rainbow trout with which we stocked the pond, but rarely fished, lived to a ripe old age in the cold, clear waters.

Surrounded by woodlands, we decided to encourage many of the living things that were already here—the birds, the frogs, the fireflies and scores of late summer chirping crickets, and the occasional wild turkeys crossing our field. I believe that we did so by retaining the best of the native vegetation while leaving plenty of room for many introduced plants.

Under the circumstances, it was easy to create interesting scenes from every window of our newly built home because the raw ingredients all fit into place. The front windows of our raised ranch house overlook the pond. Placid at times, rippling and storm-tossed at others, the surface water reveals the weather in all its moods. In winter, ice usually forms, smooth, sleek, iridescent, and usually strong enough for skating. The dam around it, planted to a sturdy field grass, is wide enough to be cut by a tractor mower, and the bordering trees as well as introduced ornamentals are seen double, their images pure in the pond waters. Sliding doors in our north facing living room open on to a raised deck-in-the-trees and also, to a good view of the field. In the distance, we can see our neighbor's meadow and his several grazing horses. The south side of the house faces the drive, and over the garage, a small greenhouse was erected. On the east side or rear of the house, below the planted hillside, is an auxiliary brook. Part of it is visible from the kitchen windows. In front of it is a small lawn, and on the far side, a grove of native trees that has been preserved. This shady spot supports a great many wildflowers.

Admittedly, the soils on the property, partially drained where necessary, needed a good deal of amending in order to grow many introduced plants. And then, too, ours is a cold little valley with frost lingering long in springtime and returning rather early in autumn. The intervening years, in which there have been many do-it-yourself garden projects, have also brought a host of small problems, and in the thirtieth year after the property was first developed, my husband and I recognized that serious renovation was needed in several areas.

One does not have to live on country acreage to enjoy attractive views. Smaller garden spaces have their own personality, and with great care, we should try to determine those qualities that we wish to add—and are within the realm of possibility. The goal should be to provide something of interest all year round, and so, whereever you live the essential element here is at least one moderate sized house window. Given even a single window, there is an opportunity for the homeowner to enjoy an outdoor scene. For the homeowner, this is a great way to employ those creative juices that we all possess.

I think of some gardens I've observed that were designed in minimal spaces. Typical are the many surrounding private homes in Japan. I think of diminutive and exceedingly pretty front and back yards in Britain and France. I think of small, Spanish courtyards, fascinating rock gardens in the Southwest, an exquisite little patio garden outside a hotel room in Hawaii, city gardens in San Francisco on tiny, hilly lots, etc., etc. Each and every garden had a single thing in common: at least one exceptional window view. It was all-important to those in residence who wanted to enjoy an attractive scene from indoors as well as outdoors, and all year long.

A great view is, of course, in the eye of the beholder. There are those who see our country garden as nothing but work, work, work, and would have none of it for themselves. There are others who feel that the only view worth having is that of a city skyline. Should they also enjoy flowers, they might be perfectly content with balcony gardening, and thus create their own "contained" garden view. Different strokes for different folks. Try this experiment: the next time you are traveling and staying overnight in a hotel, ask the desk clerk for a room with a view. It may, of course, turn out to be just that in a place where such things are possible. On one occasion, we asked for such a room and were surprised.

The clerk led us to what he considered an outstanding sight. It was a view of a parking lot filled with luxurious BMWs!

Start assessing your older garden by observing whether or not you already have created interesting window views. It's never too late to add them wherever they might be missing. Then appraise the area of your home that you use most frequently. Is it that little alcove with your desk? Or do you all too often find yourself in your kitchen? Or is it the bedroom, den, or living room to which you gravitate as a fine place to relax, snuggled down into a favorite easy chair?

I'll tell you what we did with the two side-by-side 3 ½' double hung windows in our kitchen dinette. Food, of course, draws us into the kitchen, but this is also a favorite spot for viewing our rear garden east of the house. The small lawn here, backed by a little stream and hillside, has a horse-shoe shaped bed facing the kitchen. The focal point in the bed is a splendid Japanese maple, *Acer palmatum* 'Bloodgood'. Planted at 2', it has now reached 20' in about twenty years. With any luck, it will not grow much taller! The tree displays a richness of fine foliage that is bright red in spring, then changes to burgundy in summer, and finally to crimson in autumn. A smaller, dissected leaf Japanese maple rounds off the corner. These specimens are underplanted with masses of flowering plants for each season...daffodils in early spring, followed by white flowered Japanese woodland primroses, *Primula sieboldii*, then azaleas later in spring, *Dianthus* 'Ideal Burgundy' in June, *Hosta* 'August Moon' for midsummer, and cardinal flowers for late summer to early autumn. However, the trees remain the center of interest with the other ornamentals massed below them as room allows. Even in winter, the taller maple's gray, multi stemmed trunks are attractive, and the branches cup the snow like outstretched arms. This is the way to plant, I think, when designing a garden bed: focal point complemented by mass plantings of a single species for each season.

When the other ornamentals are dormant in winter, including the bare tree and the azaleas, I wanted to add a little more interest to this rear garden scene. Clearly visible from the dinette is a feeder on a pole that attracts a great number of birds and the ever- present acrobatic squirrels. Nearby trees act as a lift-off when the birds descend to the feeder. It is especially exciting to view the frequent comings and goings of the dozen cardinals that inhabit our property. On a snowy day, the red males stand out in sharp relief to the white cover. There is nothing highly complex or unusual about this little scene from our windows, but it provides us with great joy and interest when the rest of the garden is asleep. One caution though; fallen bird seed is a sure way to kill lawn grasses. Placing the feeder in its own mulched or graveled area, at a slight distance from the planting bed, can help to avoid this problem.

Perhaps there are other features that you would prefer to see from a favorite window seat facing the rear of your home. A garden of dwarf conifers would be truly sublime, or perhaps, this is the place for that pool of recirculated water that you've wanted to create. Breaking the surface with a few water-lilies might be your choice, but keeping it clear as a reflecting pool, which mirrors the nearby flowers, is another possible treatment. The latter is how we have used our waters at Frog Pond Farm. Ponds or pools—whatever you call them--are such a lovely sight that to place them out of view from a window is a wasted resource.

Unusual trees of many kinds may be used as a focal point. A host of not-too-large trees, besides Japanese maples, could also serve that purpose. *Betula nigra* 'Heritage', for example, is the splendid river birch noted for its multicolored bark brown, beige, and cocoa colored, ever changing with the seasons. Or, perhaps, you might try the chokecherry, *Prunus maackii*, with cinnamon red bark or the paperbark maple, *Acer griseum*. Many trees noted for their dramatic flowers could also be used; one that is particularly lovely in all seasons and follows the native dogwood in bloom is *Cornus kousa*, the Korean dogwood. It has beautiful white calyxes in June and an incredibly long flowering period. This is followed by a very ornamental display of raspberry-like fruit, which, I recently discovered, is edible to man. Something that not all gardeners realize is that the Korean dogwood has a splendid mottled bark for winter interest. For our Northeastern area, it can scarcely be rivaled. Decide, when it is young, if you would prefer to see it grow with one trunk or many emerging from the ground.

The great fun of gardening is selection, but it's tempting to disregard the rules of the game. More than once, when I coveted an unusual tree and ignored its requirements, I planted it anyway—and lost it gradually. A gardener's obsession can be a roll of the dice. Sometimes, there's a big payoff. More often, there's a big loss.

Most importantly, you'll need to follow the cultural needs of all new plants in order to make appropriate selections. You can amend heavy clay soils to only a certain degree, you can hope for warmer winters until Doom's Day, you can air condition indoors when the weather is beastly hot, but you can't plant just any new plant in any old place. In the end, Mother Nature rules and if you don't follow her dictates in your selection of plants, you'll lose out in the end. If the species you want is a little unusual, you may not be able to locate it at a nearby nursery and, instead, order it mail order. The plant you receive will probably be a little smaller than you would prefer, but exercise a little patience. In a suitable location, small grows faster than we might expect. The entire process of selection, purchase, and planting should not be hurried considering the length of time you will be enjoying the fruits of your labor, especially if it will be in your view garden.

Working with the non-living parts of a landscape is called hardscaping. If your view has a good sized space in back of your house, a distant greenhouse might be just the ticket, or a vine-covered pergola, or, instead of a patio against the house, a gazebo placed at a suitable distance. If your desires and your budget do not coincide, a grouping of large, handsome, frost proof (in cold winter areas) pots or other containers would be rather nice. Or consider a simple but elegant stone bench set in an evergreen groundcover. In some places, such an addition may be all that is needed. Let your imagination be your guide, but for heaven's sake, rather than placing every feature up against the house, plot your view garden out from under. The purpose is to be able to see these features easily from the most frequently used window-side chairs in your home.

On a very level lot, you can create a great deal of interest with a change of elevation. If you are able to provide the proper drainage, and your windows enable you to look down into a special garden, consider a slightly sunken terrace at the rear of your house enclosed with retaining walls. When situated properly, a protected terrace like this might create a warm microclimate for a few spectacular but marginally hardy plants that would otherwise not thrive in your area. Or, you might want to go the other way and raise up a bump or berm of soil and plant it with attractive low growers.

On older properties, sometimes it is difficult to gain access to a rear area. However, where there's a will, there's often a way. In landscaping a client's garden many years ago, narrow side yards prevented the movement of heavy plants, materials, and machinery to the back of the house. Happily, the next-door neighbor consented to our temporarily using his driveway and removing his side yard fencing. With improvisation, and much luck, a not-too-obvious solution can sometimes be found.

Clearing away trees that are too close to a favorite window might be necessary to obtain a good view. If your tree is insect or disease prone, a chain saw can solve this problem. However, if it is in good health, you will probably hesitate before eliminating it and chose, instead, selective pruning. Do remember, though, that this very tree could be eliminating a potential hot spot against your house by shading it in the summer. This being the case, if you remove it and if your home is air conditioned, you would probably see a rise in your electric bill. If the tree is evergreen and it now shelters a cold, windy corner, removal might mean a need for more heat indoors might be necessary. So think through "your remedy" carefully. Remember that it takes but a little time to chop down a tree that may have taken a long time to grow to its present size. Then, too, if you cannot identify the tree, get an arborist to help you determine this. It might be something so uncommon and precious that destroying it would be a tragedy. In this situation, it might be best to leave well enough alone and choose another window for your garden viewing.

Minor windows of your home may also benefit from the creation of a nice view. You may rarely bother now to look out at a side yard when that yard is a passageway unused except for quick trips to the rear of the house. Where space is at a premium, you might add something exciting to see from that window. A side yard fence can support any number of ornamentals. A favorite of mine is one of the cultivars of the firethorn, *Pyracantha coccinea*, with a lovely autumn display of orange or red fruit—there is even a yellow-berried variety, although not as hardy as others. It can be pruned or espaliered flat against a so-so fence making something nice out of nothing special. Besides, there are seventeen different kinds of birds that love to feast on the berries thus adding to its interest and, in turn, increasing your insect-devouring populations. To flower and fruit, however, this shrub needs plenty of sunlight.

Another possibility for clothing a side-yard fence is a planting of one of the more elegant forms of English ivy. Some are silver dusted, others crinkly of leaf, veined in white, blotched in gold, etc. In a winter climate colder than Zone 6, some varieties may be only semi evergreen. Then, too, not all kinds are thoroughly hardy, and others mound, rather than climb, not too useful for clambering up a fence. So choose carefully. In my own Zone 5 garden, *Hedera helix* 'Duckfoot' is both hardy and very pretty, but not a very fast climber. H.h. 'Buttercup' with cream, yellow, and pale pink overtones, is lovely but also, a slow climber. It needs a sturdy support. For a fence covering in a cold area, the cultivars 'Harrison,' 'Woerner,' 'Baltica', and 'Hibernica' may be the most reliable. For the best advice whenever venturing into a horticultural area new to you, consult with experts. The American Ivy Society in Ohio can supply you with a great deal of information.

When scale insects are not a problem, various forms of *Euonymus fortunei* 'Coloratus' might be used on the fence. Winter green, with pretty fruits from August through September, it can be quite attractive. There are many variegated forms of this euonymous, but some may not have a propensity to climb. Consult with your local agricultural agent to get detailed information.

There are a host of deciduous flowering vines that can be trained on a fence but we are mostly concerned here with winter views for those who are faced each year with a bleak and dormant six month outlook. Gardeners who live in warmer climates than Zone 6 will have no trouble selecting climbers that flower almost every month of the year.

If you have a so-called picture window in your home, large glass doors, or a wall that is almost totally glass, then you already have the perfect spot from which to establish a view garden. Where several good sized windows are in place around your home, then you will, by necessity, want to vary your view garden plant selections. Arrange one spot for viewing shade loving plants, perhaps hollies or other winter fruiting ornamentals, and another area in full sun for early flowering bulbs, shrubs or perennials. It is no problem at all locating the window in your home that is the sunniest if you have a cat. In winter, that is where you can expect to find her most of the time.

When each little indoor-outdoor scene is complete, don't be surprised if you begin to investigate night lighting, just another dimension in window garden viewing. And then, you'll surely want to push back your curtains, or open your blinds, or fold clear your draperies because now, the outdoors has come indoors. What a great place to start revitalizing your garden!

CHAPTER III
GETTING DOWN TO BRASS TACKS

CHAPTER III.
Getting Down To Brass Tacks

Case history: Revamping the Border Along Our Driveway

No doubt about it. This border was in sad condition. It slopes downward slightly toward our driveway and is retained by a low wall of railroad ties varying in height between 2½ to 4'. The British call these ties "sleepers," and ours were surely laying down on the job. Instead of holding up the bank, time had pushed and shoved them forward like commuters on a busy subway. They were also rotting. This was no surprise to us since we had installed them thirty years ago. Their deteriorating condition had long been ignored but now, it really bothered us.

The principle planted area above the ties is about 25' wide and 85' in length. In back of this, water from wet woodlands captured in a ditch is sent tumbling out to the road and a catch basin. When my husband cut brush in order to install deer fencing, we were able to examine the plantings above the ties. All had become impossibly crowded; some were beyond salvaging.

We had neglected this project for many years because my attention was diverted to the other side of the drive where there is a nicely landscaped bed. But no garden space should be wasted, and I wanted to retain the raised framework of Canadian hemlocks, three lovely 'Katherine' crabapples, and a green carpet of myrtle. Quite a few cascaders softened the look of the wall but they all needed more space.

Before proceeding, we marked each plant that had to be removed starting with an upright juniper. Have you ever seen an aging Blaauw's juniper? Chances are, it has grown bare in the center (sadly, the nature of the beast). Then, too, it is one conifer that can't seem to make up its mind if it should be upright or vase shaped, and worse, it flops at peculiar angles. This juniper had to go. More than a dozen other shrubs had also aged badly.

At this point, I determined not to overplant again. When many of the old plants were removed, there might be room to add a few select new shrubs, specimens that do not grow too tall. Rhododendrons? Before it had become a planting area, the site was too hot and sunny for these broadleafs, but now, partial shade prevails, just what most of these plants prefer. Ah, yes to a few moderate height rhododendrons.

Whenever renovating an area, regardless of its size, consider the four essentials: what should remain, what should be removed, what should be rebuilt and what should be replanted. That is the thinking process behind all restorations:

1. REMAIN: The hemlocks and crabapples in this raised bed would stay.

Canadian hemlocks, with their slender, drooping branches, were once a common woodland tree in this area through the millennia, and they deserve to be cherished. Unfortunately, woolly adelgid has become a serious insect threat to this species in many places although not yet a problem here. Hopefully, the pestilence will run its course before it reaches us. We will keep a sharp eye out for it. The crabs, themselves, needed some corrective pruning plus fertilizing with tree spikes to encourage healthy new growth.

As we removed some of the undesirable plants, we discovered three large, hidden 'Palestrina' azaleas. Under the right conditions, without smothering shrubs and weeds around them, these azaleas are froths of white blossoms in May. Now, given ample room, they would remain and flourish. And they did!

Finally, the groundcover of myrtle *(Vinca minor)* needed to be increased. In places, it grew lush and green, but some topsoil had washed away taking patches of the myrtle with it. We would address this problem last.

2. REMOVE: Our railroad tie wall obviously needed replacement as did the few tie steps and a stretch of wall extending to the house. We considered substituting a dry laid natural stone wall, and that would have been splendid. My husband and I had constructed these rock walls elsewhere on our property when we first arrived here, and we still had a ready supply of boulders along our roadsides. Unfortunately, the two of us are no longer strong enough nor ambitious enough to deal with them ourselves on a large project. Skilled mason labor for such an extensive an area is so expensive that we immediately ruled that out.

The new paver rocks (they look like stone but are really concrete) were another possibility, a little less labor intensive, thus, less costly, than native rocks. However, I decided that their appearance was too formal for our naturalistic garden.

In the country of New Zealand, we had observed many kinds of walls constructed of broken concrete slabs removed from old flooring. The walls look amazingly like natural flagstone. The problem, of course, is to locate a good supply when you need it. For us, in a rural area, it never was a choice we could consider.

Machine milled timbers for retaining walls are now available treated with non-arsenic preservatives such as an organic fungicide. They are probably the safest lumber to use near a water supply, children's play space, or vegetable garden. Yet, where none of these situations apply, there is something to be said in favor of the woodsy look of railroad ties, especially in a garden well endowed with trees. They do, indeed, make splendid looking garden walls. Much of the creosote originally used to preserve the ties has leached away by the time they are removed and sold to gardeners. Twenty-five or thirty years is about what one can expect from them before decay sets in.

Eventually, we settled for hiring a contractor to remove the old and install the new ties. We insisted—and got—the best quality that could be found, ties that were old, clean, yet rugged looking. There was scarcely a sign of decay.

Do-it-yourselfers cannot resist participating to some extent in such a project, and so, while waiting for the contractor, we pulled out the old shrubbery. Some of it was merely cut away at the surface. The rest had heavy trunks and extensive root systems. If you, as a homeowner, are faced with this situation, you should be able to handle large plants if you cut them down to size. We accomplished the removals by first chopping some of the unwanted shrubs into manageable pieces with loppers, then cutting each one down with a chain saw leaving 2 to 3' of trunk. We fastened a chain around the trunk and hooked the other end of the chain to our car. Slowly moving forward with one great lurch, the entire plant landed in our driveway.

If you leave stumps behind and have them ground down by a hired stump grinder, be warned. These machines can create quite a bit of air borne dust and debris which might linger for awhile.

The most bothersome of our removals were several blue hollies (*Ilex x meserveae* 'Blue Boy' and 'Blue Girl'). When planted years ago, these cultivars had just been introduced and they were called dwarfs! Lovely as they were, in the twenty years of their placement here, they grew 8-10', and almost as broad. I was about to prune and possibly transplant them when I discovered that small pieces had root run here and there over the entire area. With my goal of creating a low maintenance garden, invasive plants like these had to go. After the hollies were cut down, all their running roots were dug out by hand.

A job like this is bound to generate a considerable amount of brush. If yours is a city or suburban property with no convenient place for a large brush pile, or if your community doesn't have brush collection, you may want to locate a tree company that will turn all your prunings into woodchips. No more useful commodity can come out of your garden, and even if you must make room for temporary storage, partially decayed chips are valuable for use as a mulch. When well rotted, they make an excellent soil amendment.

The next step was delayed as we waited for the contractor to tear down the old wall and install the new. Meanwhile, with the assistance of our occasional helper, we balled and burlapped about a dozen shrubs that were well worth transplanting. The cascaders, including several *Cotoneasters* 'Coral Beauty,' 3 large Nakahari azaleas, and some arching spiraeas, were set aside for the finished planting. There would be no sunny space for our weeping shrub rose, but not wishing to discard it, the rose was transplanted into a partially shady place above the ties—and it still blooms amazingly well!

After clearing the area of unwanted plants, I was now able to hand weed in order to get rid of seedling perennial pests..ash and maple, barberry, burning bush, oriental bittersweet, multiflora roses, ground ivy, poison ivy, and even some dodder. I generally use a trowel with a long, narrow, tapered blade. Unfortunately, merely digging out perennial or broad-leaf weeds, if they are more than a few inches tall, is not always sufficient. No matter how thoroughly you attack them, most will grow again from splinter roots. These plants I spot sprayed with a contact systemic herbicide containing glyphosate (I used "Roundup"). It leaves no residue in the soil but must be applied on a windless day to prevent drift onto other plants. Use it only when rainfall is not expected for at least 6 hours.

If your weeds are mostly grasses and annuals, gardeners who prefer a more organic approach may have to hand weed, or you might try a product, soon to be available, called Organic Interceptor. Made from pine trees planted throughout the North Island of New Zealand, this weed controller breaks down cell walls so that they dehydrate. The manufacturer claims that it also suppresses the top growth of many perennial species, but waxy stems and leaves, as well as stoloniferous rooted weeds, are harder to eliminate. On other types, it is claimed that Interceptor is highly effective.

3. REBUILD: By mid-June, the contractor arrived and quickly, with the help of a backhoe and several men, removed and loaded the old ties onto their truck. If you should find yourself with a large quantity of debris, do not be surprised at the high but necessary cost of trucking and dump disposal.

The most important aspect of installing railroad ties is proper drainage. A retaining wall acts as a dam holding back soil during every heavy rainfall. After placing the first tier of ties into a shallow ditch, the contractors drilled weep holes here and there to allow an exit for excessive water. While the men were working, we moved to the rear of the border where a drainage ditch catches excessive rainfall from our wet woodland. The ditch was cleared of soggy leaves and deepened slightly to better direct the water down to the road.

Building retaining walls higher than 3' may require a building permit from your town or city. Check to make sure. We watched as the workers set staggered joints of ties one over the other using strings and a level to assure that they sit without wobbling. After the first tier, the rest were set to lean back slightly into the bank. The ties were further anchored with rebars (reinforcing rods) or spikes and ample "dead men" (underground ties) were occasionally placed at right angles to the wall. As each tier was completed, a sandy, gravelly material was packed behind it. All in all, it is a job that requires experience, so choose your contractor carefully.

4. REPLANT: At last, the time had come to transplant those specimens that had been set aside. Unfortunately, it was already mid-June and getting a little warm here for the best results. In the real world, you can almost expect contractor delays, and we had to wait for

the new wall to be in place before resetting the plants. The root balls of the transplants, carefully watered, looked none the worse for the elapsed time. We kept a hose handy in the driveway during this period despite its untidy appearance. When working on jobs such as this, I heed the words of my husband who always says: "You can't make an omelet without cracking eggs."

If you can possibly anticipate moving special plants, it is far better to root prune each specimen a year in advance. Do this by cutting around the root circumference of the plant with a sharp spade and then leave it where it sits until it is ready to be dug and transplanted. Rhododendrons and azaleas, because of their fibrous root systems, seldom need this treatment. With other woodies, it offers a kind of insurance, especially when the plants have been growing for a long time in one spot. The trickiest specimen that we transplanted was a dwarf Montgomery spruce (*Picea pungens* 'R.H. Montgomery') that had been growing not so dwarf in the gravely soil of my rock garden. It is next to impossible to create a sturdy ball of earth in this kind of soil, so we could not root prune it before hand, but the little spruce was eventually dug out with as much care as possible and it survived intact.

At last, we could plant six new all-of-a-kind rhododendrons (for a mass effect), spaced as naturally as possible within the planting bed. This was followed by transplanting the cascaders just above the ties giving them plenty of growing space. We amended a large area under and around the new plantings with a mixture of compost and peat moss to achieve good results, and in addition, the entire bed was spread with 6 cubic yards of spent mushroom compost that had been supplied by the contractor. A gardener cannot expect good results unless soil fertility is adequate.

The final step meant filling in the area with more groundcover plants of myrtle *(Vinca minor)* in places where they had formerly washed away. About 2000 new clumps were needed set on 8" centers.

After I filled in all the bare spots with the myrtle, merely the thought of hand weeding again that season had me frazzled. And so, I decided to use a pre-emergent herbicide on the entire area. Unfortunately, it is difficult to find a pre-emergent that is recommended as safe for myrtle, but I used a granular product called "Preen" labeled for annual grasses and groundcovers. The manufacturer does, indeed, list his product as non harmful when used on myrtle, or periwinkle as it is sometimes called. For a first time use, however, they do recommend testing one plant for 30 to 60 days, but I blew caution to the winds and applied it immediately, 1 ounce for every 10 sq. feet, watered in immediately, but without the necessity of cultivating it into the soil. Luck was with me and weed suppression that first season was more than adequate. If your planting is followed by a very hot summer, you might have to reapply it again in a few months.

Although organic gardeners usually scoff at the use of chemicals saying that they damage the environment, I'd venture to say that many, if not most, experienced horticulturists tending large, public gardens, use herbicides occasionally. If carefully handled, they are indispensable for suppressing weeds. Were they not safe, herbicides of all kinds would surely be outlawed. Then, too, since many of our worst weeds originated in far off places, we are not starting with an uncorrupted situation. Like it or not, virgin areas are few and far between; the natural landscape has already been changed.

Whatever large project you are involved in, it is, of course, economical to do part of the work yourself if at all possible. Do-it-yourselfers will have a greater feeling of accomplishment with the finished result if they participate to some degree. Placing your own fingers in the pie will give you the feeling that the best result possible has been achieved.

I have described this entire procedure in some detail because it is rather typical of many landscape renovation projects—remain, remove, rebuild, and replant. Even if you hire others to do the entire job, it's a good idea to know exactly what they are about. How else can you be a competent judge?

CHAPTER IV

THAT SPACE IN FRONT OF YOUR HOUSE

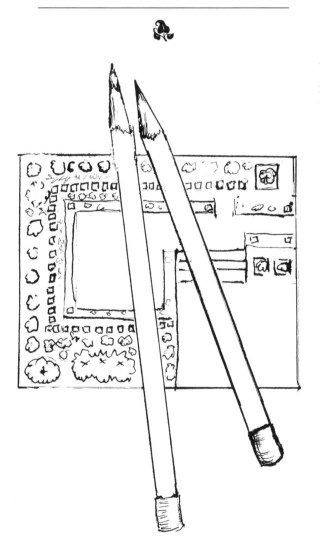

CHAPTER IV.
That Space In Front Of Your House

Who says that plants are mute? If not an audible voice, perhaps they have their own sign language. Do brambles along your front path scratch at your legs with every passing? Or are those vines smothering your frame house warning you, with rotting timbers, that they are ready to return wood to earth? Or is that shrub covering your water spigot developing yellow leaves? It might be telling you that it cannot stand another drip, drip, drip. Plants can soothe and plants can please but they can also damage our man-created structures. What some of yours may be saying is "remove us or else."

Chances are, if your foundation planting has been in place longer than seventeen years, it needs redoing. This is especially obvious when the front door and windows are shrouded with shrubs. As distressing as it might be to contemplate, your front path also might have seen better days. Degraded construction materials, such as cracked flagstones or crumbling bricks or concrete, may be just as unattractive-and unsafe-as overgrown plantings.

Can your house be easily located from the street by all visitors? Maybe what it lacks is individuality, the visual magnet that distinguishes one building from another in a neighborhood. This is often the case where the builder constructed all the houses on a block from one set of blueprints. If you are concerned with the future resale value of your house, then a good first impression is needed to distinguish your home as unique and charming. It goes a long way toward convincing observers that "this house is special." Be of good cheer because imaginative landscaping can sometimes do this.

You, who are now set on revitalizing your property, should remember that future buyers may not be able to discern great plants from lackluster varieties but they will certainly notice pleasing design and good-looking construction. Yes, I, too, am always in a hurry to consider plants above all else, but before removing and replacing them, realize that this is also the time to correct any faults in the hardscaping–those non-living parts of the landscape that are necessary to the realization of a lovely framework for your house.

Why wait for your property to come up for sale before creating anew? I think of a family on country acreage who commissioned me to draw up plans for a large deck at the front of their south-facing house. Besides sunning themselves, they wanted the deck to improve their downward sloping, poorly designed entranceway. I drew the plans. They liked them. Yet, they put off construction until a few months before their house was sold. Sadly, this family had only a very brief time in which to enjoy their new deck.

If you've never before worked with an overall landscape plan on paper, then you will probably be surprised at how helpful and reassuring it is. It allows you, the homeowner, a whole range of treatments in this most "public" part of your property—treatments that you may never have imagined by merely looking at the site. Yet, some gardeners design by the seat of their pants, with a plan in their heads rather than in their hands. I think, though, that it is more luck than skill if they are able to fit all the renovated parts into a well coordinated whole. It has often been said how much easier it is to erase an image on paper than to move a tree. That is the purpose of a landscape plan! No matter how simple or complex the project, there are almost always many options to consider in creating a satisfactory scheme. Hopefully, the plan that you draw for yourself will take into consideration all your wants, your needs, and your available funds. Or, if you prefer, call in a competent landscape designer or architect to offer you his best version.

If you leave the design in the hands of a landscape contractor rather than a designer, he or she must be able to fully share it with you. More often than not, he will merely tell you what he is going to do, perhaps draw a simple sketch, and then follow this with an estimate of costs. If you accept his plan on such a sketch, and he proceeds with the construction, you may very well like his results. Then again, the sketch may be too skimpy to show you the complete picture. If you are not pleased with the design, ask him to add whatever details that bother you, and he may be able to comply.

You might have many areas at the front of your house that are already well designed but need plant renovation. If you are a do-it-yourself gardener, you can usually handle this by yourself. However, if redesign and/or hardscaping is involved and complicated problems must be remedied, you actually have several choices:

1. Work with a contractor who has a design-on-paper staff member.

2. Employ a landscape architect or designer whose finished work you greatly admired. He or she will be able to draw up partial or complete plans for you and then, either set you up with an experienced crew or recommend one or more contractors. Both contractors and architects should be able to give you cost estimates.

3. If you have some really definite ideas about how you want your front entrance to look (with suggestions throughout this book) why not experiment yourself by drawing your own plan on paper? How else can you fully describe such matters as a new path that you want to zig where now it zags? Yes, there are many talented landscape architects and designers who will be exceedingly sensitive to your ideas, but there is also the fun and satisfaction to be had from doing it yourself—if your property is not too complex.

A landscape plan is like a road map. It will help you to decide how best to get from your starting point to your destination and to avoid the detours that will set you off course. You should know, before you start, that the materials and techniques mentioned below for drawing up a plan are merely a summary of the entire design making process. For a property that is large or needs a major overhaul, there are many fine references that can be studied before you begin. (See "Recommended Reading") However, the following points will give you a good idea of what is involved, and if you want to give it a try, it's not a bad idea to begin with your front entrance development:.

The mechanics of creating your own landscape plan are not really difficult if you have the right tools: a 100' tape measure, stakes, two or three large sheets of drafting paper, several straight-edges, medium-lead pencils, a good eraser, one or two French curves, several size circle templates for trees and shrubs, and an architect's ruler with a scale of ½, ¼ , or ⅛th of an inch to indicate each foot. The ¼ of an inch will probably be adequate for most average sized front-of-yard landscaping.

When drawing all measurements in your chosen scale, first put in place the boundary lines of your property using your surveyor's plot plan. If you cannot find it, your township probably has a copy. Next, place your house on the plan. Break the drawing down to the front entrance area only if that is what you now want to change. Then, take on-the-ground measurements, drawing, in scale, the sizes and shapes of all existing elements including the lawn, the shade trees, the ornamental plants, and the location of your existing steps, walls, paths, windows, and doors. Use your circle templates to approximate the size of each existing tree or shrub. Slopes and valleys are difficult to measure if you are not a surveyor, but an arrow up or down will help you to keep in mind uneven terrain. You can add the driveway, too, if it will be part of the newly devised scheme. Be sure to mark the location of fences, walls, underground utilities, water connections, or anything else that might be affected. Note the views, if any, that you wish to preserve, or anything that you'd just as soon conceal. Decide, from the outset, the best areas to place a view garden (See Chapter II) if windows at the front of your residence encourage such a feature. Measuring the width of the windows and their distance above grade is also very important so that a new planting will not block them.

If you do not already know the exposure, use a compass to find out. Also indicate prevailing winds. Both exposure and wind velocity may very well affect your choice of plants.

When the sketch is complete, do an overlay to work out your proposed changes. Now is the time to create a repositioned path, if that is what you want, plus an edging that might be necessary. Then indicate the lawn and/or ground cover with short perpendicular lines. Any code, really, that you choose to use will be satisfactory.

Last, but not least, decide on the plants that must be removed, those that will remain, and any new ones that you want to add. To indicate the placement of all new (or retained) shrubs and trees, use templates of varying sizes, and place within each abbreviations of the plant names. Be certain that the distance between new and old plants allows for growth, at least during the next ten years. Indicate planting beds with diagonal slash lines which you will later erase and fill with more abbreviated names.

While plotting your front entrance plan, here are some other points to consider:

Front Door:

Are you one of those people who enters your house through the garage, rear, or side door? Your route is probably the shortest distance between two points, a situation you want to preserve for those times when your arms are overflowing with groceries. However, when the principal door seems invisible to your guests, it may be due to the fact that:

1. they are in a rush and seeking the fastest entry, or
2. the front path and possibly, steps, are not comfortable, safe, and attractive, or
3. the doorway cannot easily be seen because it is blocked by vegetation

The invisible front door is a typical design blunder. Why? Because this is the door that usually opens to an entrance hall which leads to a living room (the most gracious part of your house), rather than a work room, mud room, or kitchen. It is the place where you want guests to get the best first impression of your home. Make it a great impression.

Merely removing the excess vegetation outside will improve things, but more can be done to accent the positive. Consider the house that has two doors at the front. To be sure, the one closest to the drive gets the most use. If, however, if you have a secondary door and it is the nearest entrance to the drive, it might take a bit of clever manipulating to entice the visitor to use the primary door. For example, try this:

Design a path and plantings that beckon the visitor onward toward the door that you want them to use. While doing this, de-emphasize the secondary door possibly by painting it the same color as the house. Then, accent the formal door. Several methods will do the trick. You might add a decorative molding above or around this door and paint it a distinctive color. Or, above the door, you might construct a portico or roofed porch to protrude over the entrance. Or, if the landing is wide enough, you might build permanent planter boxes on each side and keep them filled with seasonal flowers or greenery. Painting the door a contrasting color will also call attention to it.

Proportion, Balance, and Style:

There are few things more unsettling than a house that looks uncomfortable on its lot. Like a boy putting on man's clothes or a man squeezing into boy's clothing, a poor fit is disconcerting to all. A large house on too small a lot, a small house on a large and empty lot, a moderate-sized house with heavy trees and shrubbery on one side and a bare look on the other—all are examples of poor scale and proportion. If your property suffers from similar problems, you might wish that you could lift up your old house and move it to a better location on your lot. Not only is such a drastic solution unwarranted, if not impossible, but good landscape design can often conceal or modify this kind of problem. What the designer must do is to create an illusion of balance by carefully judging the planting mass on each side of the house. Except in a formal garden, these may not be the same plants, but they should be a selection that gives weight where it is needed. A heavy planting of trees and shrubbery on one side of a house might best be thinned if there is simply no room on the other side for equal weight. It may be that changing the location of your front path or adding some special feature to increase a needed mass, might help to balance the whole. Hard and fast rules are difficult to make because there are so many variables, but you will be able to better decide what is a lopsided effect and where either more or less is needed. Then make the needed changes on your site plan.

Coordinating the landscaping with the house style is also important. It will help you to decide whether a formal, symmetrical design or a more informal, asymmetrical arrangement will look best to achieve good balance throughout your front-of-house design.

Many formal, traditional house styles such as most Colonials, Federal, Italianate, Georgian, Greek Revival, or Victorians, usually have central door placement on the house often with equal-sized windows on each story. It is this symmetry that should be repeated in the landscape design if you wish to retain that distinctive style. However, be forewarned: same sized, same species ornamentals may be very difficult to maintain because few plants grow at the same rate of speed. And, should one plant die, replacing it with a matching specimen could be difficult. Nevertheless, it is important to achieve a symmetry of plantings which will help to lend this architectural style a feeling of order and preservation.

On the other hand, with more contemporary architecture, such as a split-level or a raised ranch plus Tudor, and other styles in imitation of many in Europe, the asymmetrical arrangement of hardscaping and plantings might be more fitting. However, American homes today are an amalgamation of styles. If this describes your house, when you renovate your front entrance, you will have to use your own judgment in deciding the look that best suits you.

Another concept to consider is scale. Think of a small woman wearing a large chunk of jewelry. It may be worth a king's ransom, but it is totally out of proportion to her petite dimensions. Think of a portly gentleman wearing a wide tie over his broad chest. It looks right somehow because the scale is right. A skinny tie on him would make him look like a comedian.

Good proportion is when all parts are considered in relationship to the whole. An example of poor architectural proportion is when a walk that is 3' wide fronts a massive three-story Georgian style. Compared with the size of the house, the walk looks like a wormy ribbon even though 3' is wide enough for two not-too-large persons to walk abreast. Its proportion, in relation to the house, is all wrong. In front of a small cottage, 4' of width may be quite enough. Pathways as wide as 6 to 8' are appropriate in front of a very large house, especially if it is two or more stories high.. Narrow pathways have their place, those that twine and twist amid the most intimate sections of a rear garden, but if you wish to convey a warm and welcoming appearance at the threshold of your large home, be generous with the size of your paths.

One of the great advantages of the wide pathway is that it permits the growth of plants on one or both sides without them tearing at your arms, legs, or clothing. It is exceedingly pleasant to walk along a path bordered by interesting ornamentals, and in fact, is one of the garden-minded homeowner's favorite areas.

The importance of good proportion and proper scale was brought home to me quite clearly when I was once asked to landscape a moderate-sized house. In front was a central path with two very large shade trees--I believe that they were both London planes-- on both sides of the walk. The trees dominated the site, as there was no more than 60' of width in front of the house. To make matters worse, the homeowner insisted on growing turfgrass here. The owner had seeded over and over again adding fresh topsoil each time. He then had a landscape company plant sod, but that, too, petered away. It was obvious that the roots of the two trees sucked up all available moisture. When I parted from my client, he was still struggling with the problem because he would not consider the obvious solution—cutting down the trees. In time, they would have to be removed anyway since they can grow to a height of 100' and might endanger the house if a large limb tumbled down on the roof. It is difficult to part with well-loved landmarks such as those mature trees, but without them, the house would take on a refreshingly clean appearance with the scale vastly improved.

The Principal Path:

When judging the attractiveness of your steps and paths, ask yourself whether or not they repeat the materials of the house itself. For example, a stone faced dwelling with a red brick path is as tranquil as a storm at sea. In my opinion, red brick looks out of place when combined with fieldstone. (There are, though, very mellow earth-tone colored bricks that look better). If the paved path must be redone entirely, further consider color compatibility. While I do not always like concrete walks, a wealth of imprinted blocks is available today for patios and pathways that is quite handsome. They are available in good variety, and you should be able to find colors, shapes, and textures that blend with the facade of your house. Wooden decking is another possibility. It is particularly useful if the present walk is much lower and wetter than your lawn area. Decking can raise the walk slightly higher than the lawn making a dry pathway.(See Chapter IX)

When the front of your property is very small, with a driveway on one side, consider eliminating an existing lawn entirely. Here is one way to accomplish this: provide a generous-sized paved platform from the drive to the front door. Then, to provide privacy, create full planting beds, perhaps 5 or 6' wide, around the perimeter of your front property but with plants no taller than 6 to 8'. You might design this area with lines that echo one of the bays or breaks in the house itself. Then plant the area between the platform and planting area with a low groundcover. Miss your lawn? If so, devote plenty of space for one at the rear of your home.

Your front path probably begins at the street or some place along your driveway, or possibly bordering a circular drive. A lawn divided by a central walk commonly accompanies the first. This seems to be best adapted to the formal, geometrically arranged plantings of a symmetrical style house. If that is not the look that you want, consider widening the area adjacent to the driveway with a broad landing strip, and then creating a new path running horizontal to the house.

But to be practical, this may not be a viable option for you, and, in fact, you probably will not want to consider such a change if the condition and materials of your present path are quite respectable. Where heaving and cracking have occurred in concrete, you will probably have to hire a contractor to repair or replace the original material. If you wish, you might want to have him redo the entire walk Or if your path is constructed of sand embedded flags or bricks, this may mean merely digging up a few wobbly slabs, leveling the surface below by adding crushed stone for stability, and then resetting the pavers level with the rest of the path.

Unorthodox Arrangements:

Our own front path of heavy bluestone (on a corner lot in a secluded location) is more than just a path. It begins at the drive, arches out in front of the house in a horseshoe shape, then continues down and around the north side of the house as a sitting area or patio. It has proven to be quite useful in this place where there is much privacy, and is a splendid place for summering my many container plants which are arranged on the broad steps of the house, in the arch, and on the patio, itself. Connecting the front walk with a side-of-the-house patio may prove to be feasible where there is more room on the side than in the rear. However, after three decades, a few of our bluestones heave from time to time and need to be reset. They were originally placed in sand, something I would no longer recommend because in midsummer, this material acts as a perfect home for weeds and mosses.

The mosses (on the shady side) in the cracks are quite attractive of themselves, but very difficult to maintain when the path needs to be swept or raked. A gasoline powered vacuum blower is a good tool for this purpose, and less damaging to the mosses, but autumn leaf drop is so heavy here that raking, too, is necessary.

Of course, those enamored with the cottage garden look might prefer a gravely mixture between the slabs and plant the cracks with thyme, dianthus, arenarias, or any manner of sturdy flowering groundcover. Do remember, though, that if you have many large trees overlooking the area, your patio will require careful leaf raking in the fall to prevent damage to these plants. Sometimes, we'll see a photo in a book or magazine of a design that really appeals to us. Although an imaginative solution, such as plant crack fillers, can often give an outstanding result, you may no longer be young and energetic, or you might have a busy and demanding life outside the garden which would result in having little time to establish this kind of planting. If either is true, think twice about any project that would surely increase your landscape maintenance.

Were we to construct our path and patio again, we would use rock dust instead of sand beneath and between the spaces of the individual flags. This material allows excess moisture to move below pavers into the subsoil without bringing up excessive sand. And, possibly, we might look into some of the new weed-controlling fabrics that are now being manufactured for this purpose. Today's landscapers have available to them a type of fabrics called geotextiles, something I would certainly have used if it had been on the market years ago. While allowing moisture to seep through the material, it will, at the same time, separate the below-grade materials used in a paved area and also, prevent infestations of weeds.

Stumbling Blocks:

A level path contributes to a feeling of security, and that is of paramount importance in your entranceway. If there is a distinct change of elevation along your path, and at present, you have more or less of a ramp, consider replacing it by adding a few steps. Two or more steps are so obvious that they help avoid instablity (if well lit for nighttime use) but where only one is necessary, make it clearly visible by planting the cracks below it with a groundcover such as myrtle. Each step should be about 6" high. Steps that are too shallow can be a stumbling block; overly high steps add additional strain on leg muscles.

Once in awhile, when examining an older landscape development, I have come upon a mature tree that has encroached upon a pathway. In many cases, the tree roots have pushed through the surface and could cause a walker to stumble. If the tree is to remain, the path must be widened considerably. Without disturbing the level at which the tree is growing, a broad circle of pathway around it may solve the problem. A mulch of an inch or two over the exposed roots should not cause any problem. Whatever you do, paths themselves should be almost level. To avoid possible puddling after severe rainfall, however, pitch them ever so slightly toward the street side.

In some places, surfacing rocks or boulders can also obstruct a level pathway. What once was an underlay has now become an overlay. That is Mother Nature's way in rocky places. Why fight it? Widen the path around it and leave them in place, possibly adding a few more rocks as a special indigenous feature of your area. Don't go overboard, though, and try to decorate with rock plants. A rock garden is a splendid feature but its diminutive plants need a special naturalistic setting for them to be effective.

Driveways:

Just a word about driveway design: If your drive is satisfactory, then it probably provides both off-street parking for a few cars and an adequate turn-around. As far as my own taste is concerned, the residential property devoted to excessive parking space is a waste of natural resources. Man has already used asphalt to pave over large areas of the earth, and there are probably those who would eliminate every existing vegetated area—if they could. Home, after all, is a sanctuary; let it be as green and growing as we can make it. If you're in love with paving, then move to an apartment complex or condo that has its own large parking lot. If your present driveway is not quite satisfactory, a better design is in order. When total driveway reconstruction is necessary, an architect or engineer should be consulted for a superior result. He or she will try to arrange it so that one space is devoted to a turn-around if it does not already have this feature. Backing out onto a road is a practice that is both tedious and dangerous.

Drainage:

Have you been tolerating anemic plant specimens on the corners of your house? Chances are that every time it rains, they are being drowned by run-off from your downspouts. It goes without saying that before installing new plants, drainage problems should be solved. If you've grown weary of cleaning leaves out of your roof gutters, this may be the time to remove those gutters and substitute a drip area adjacent to the foundation. Dig a ditch parallel to your house just below the eaves. Lay drainage pipe or tiles in the ditch and then cover with gravel in an area about 2' in width. Connect the end of the underground pipe to a lower area, perhaps below the lawn. Be sure to surface the ditch with a gravel that blends with the path or house itself.

If you decide to retain the downspouts, you might want to cover them with the new Semi-circular or Half Round Trellis as its also called. It is constructed of 8 gauge galvanized steel wire bent into three semi-circular sections. Each is 36" long. Place one on the top of the other, and then plant the base of the downspout with a lovely vine. It is a method that creates a pleasing feature out of a necessity, and that is all to the good when landscaping.

Some properties have such a high water table and poor percolation of water through heavy clay soils that they may need far more of a drainage system than the average homeowner can do himself. I think that this is especially true on new home grounds because those on older properties usually have solved these problems years ago. But maybe not. Maybe, through the years, you've been suffering with periods of excessive rainfall that backs up through your house foundation and into your basement. If this describes your situation, then all your new landscape efforts will be in jeopardy. It's time to call in an expert to remedy the situation. Look for one in your telephone directory under "Drainage Contractor."

Hopefully, when you are ready to redo your foundation planting, you will incorporate a view garden from one of your windows. If this is not feasible, a more traditional foundation planting can be quite satisfactory. In the next chapter, journey with me as we explore a variety of planting ideas for the threshold of your home.

CHAPTER V
REPLANTING THOSE SPACES IN FRONT OF YOUR HOUSE

Natalia Petrianyk

CHAPTER V.
Replanting Those Spaces In Front of Your House

Over forty years ago, I was faced with landscaping our first small suburban home. There were, in those days, door-to-door nursery salesmen who bombarded homeowners with glorious color photos of full-blown roses, billowing vines, and flowering shrubs. I suspect that some of those photos were taken in the temperate climate of England, or perhaps, in a part of the U.S. with a milder climate and longer growing season than in Northern New Jersey. Not realizing this, I placed an order with the salesman; it included ten hybrid tea roses for the front of our house. After planting, I realized that our 3' high concrete foundation was not covered. Then, too, during that first winter, those roses looked to me like nothing more than inert broomsticks. As soon as possible, I ripped them out and replaced them with a hemlock on each side of the house and pfitzer junipers under the windows. In short order, the concrete disappeared behind a sea of green. However, a few years later, the sea became a torrent, and in short order, the house appeared to be drowning in branches and foliage. All this growth could only be kept at bay with frequent and heavy pruning. The result was the same assemblage of contorted shapes that one sees all over our country because most homeowners, and many professional landscapers as well, use species ill fitted for foundation plantings.

Surely, there must be a better way, I thought, and then enrolled in a school of landscape design to find that way.

We Americans usually opt for a traditional foundation scheme when there is an exposed concrete house foundation, not something of beauty, and that is often the reason homeowners are eager to cover it with fast growing plants. Happily, fewer homes are being built today with unsightly foundation walls, but if your older home has this "problem" area, it is best solved by regrading, bringing the soil higher at the house level and gradually sloping it down to the yard or lawn. Although it may mean transplanting most of the foundation plants, it is a permanent solution.

Where the foundation wall is not a problem, planting the area directly below it with a simple groundcover, and then incorporating a "view garden" out from the house, will give you a pleasing variety of plant shapes and forms. Or: Arrange a traditional foundation scheme in areas with a long, winter dormant season. This means the use of slow growing vertical plantings on the corners of the house, low shrubs or groundcovers beneath the windows, and compact, mounded plants on each side of the door to emphasize its location. It's still not a bad way to go, and it does avoid what I would call "show-off" displays—too many one-of-a-kind specimens, as though the landscaper wanted to show off his horticultural acuity rather than create a pleasing framework for the house. Repetition is soothing; too much variation creates restlessness.

As a substitute for a vertical evergreen upright on each corner, I prefer seeing small flowering trees underplanted with low shrubs or a groundcover, but give the tree plenty of space--at least 20-25' from the house. Then, too, extended planting corners, where there is room, will give every house a broader, more substantial appearance. Perhaps for you, the revitalizing gardener, there is one thing that cannot be stressed too strongly and that is, even if the effect looks a little sparse for the first year or two, ornamentals in front of a foundation need to be planted out and away from the house wall, 2 ½'-3' at least. Pinched, squeezed, needing frequent shearing—that is the fate of many plants because the gardener was unable to imagine that even those with moderate growth rates might soon require more space than can be envisioned at the outset.

There's also nothing wrong with placing a few low deciduous shrubs along with conifers, but choose them with care so that, at the very least, they have colorful autumn foliage and/or colorful fruit, as well as spring or summer flowers. Broadleaf evergreens for partial shade are other possibilities; many of them, such as R. 'Purple Gem', would look nice in front of a not-too-large house. However, these small leaved "lepidote" types (covered with small, scurfy scales) do require a fair bit of sun. Many large-leafed rhododendrons, for shadier areas, often grow too tall for a foundation planting. Besides, in the greater part of our country, their magnificent evergreen foliage often looks sad on a cold winter's day when their leaves turn inward. It's a forlorn and dejected sight, like homeless folk on a city street--but it has a purpose. The large, curled leaves serve as protection from desiccation during the worst of the weather. Sheltering them with burlap is unattractive. Save their planting for a shady nook or, transplant them off center of your window view. Then, in the severest cold weather, you will not stare out at them where they appear hunched up and shivering.

To fit a not-too-high house foundation, there are many wonderful slow growing dwarf conifers that scarcely require pruning at all if spaced properly. A far greater variety of cultivars is available today than ever before, many of which might be costly to purchase since they take a long time for nurserymen to raise them into landscape-sized specimens. But the higher price is worth it because the time you save in forever pruning and transplanting will be your own! Look to specialty nurseries for the greatest selection.

It is well to realize that to have conifers grow well, you will not be able to plant them just anywhere. Most of them require full sun! This is especially true of firs (Abies), pines (Pinus), and junipers (Juniperus). Sometimes, the front foundation planting will have an area that is only modestly shaded. In this case, look to spruce (Picea), arborvitae (Thuja), and yews (Taxus). Hemlocks (Tsuga), as well as the plum yew (Cephalotaxus), two genera that should flourish in either sun or light shade. There are many lovely dwarf forms of all these conifers.

One mistake that one often sees in foundation plantings is the use of conifers that are unattractive in the winter. The rather recently introduced species of Siberian carpet cypress, *Microbiota decussata*, is low and spreading and a good shade substitute for ground-cover junipers. Its silvery gray needles look elegant in the summer. However, it does turn a rather dull brown in winter. When a conifer is to be planted close at hand, make sure that its dormant season color pleases you.

Before going plant shopping, consider the American Conifer Society's growth tables: plants growing 1-3" per year maturing at 2-3' are called miniatures; dwarfs grow 3-6" per year to a ten year height of 3-6'; intermediates, 6-12" per year eventually reaching a height of 6-15'; large, 12" per year becoming about 15' in a decade. Obviously, if you plan on being in your house for at least a decade and hope that your revitalized plantings will look handsome for at least that much time, you should search for useful slow growing forms. The term "micro conifer" has been suggested for plants that grow less than an inch per year, but it's probably best to leave those for alpine or rock gardeners to consider.

Future growth in scale with the size of your home might best be thought of in this way: if you live in a cottage, you would eventually feel crowded if you selected a Saint Bernard puppy dog as your house pet. On the other hand, a small terrier might seem rather lost in a large, rambling house. Thoroughbred plants, like thoroughbred pets, need accurate labels to give clues to their future growth. Without this information, you may be in for a surprise just like the one that accompanies ownership of a mongrel pup. It can be a wonderful pet, but its ultimate size is anybody's guess.

It is well to know that a species such as one labeled Swiss mountain pine, *Pinus mugo*, or even *P.m. pumilio*, was probably grown from seed, which means that its ultimate height cannot be predicted accurately. Ornamentals grown from cuttings or grafts are usually more reliable. Plant labels or garden center employees may not have this information, but you can be more or less certain that when the label is marked with a botanical name, you will have a good idea of its future growth. For example, if you have a small house and a low foundation in a sunny area, and you'd like to grow horizontal shaped conifers in front of it that grow no more than 2-3" per year, look for cultivars such as the dwarf balsam fir (*Abies balsamea* 'Nana'), the pygmy spruce (*Picea abies* 'Pygmaea'), the creeping spruce (*Picea abies* 'Repens'), or the low Scot's pine (*Pinus sylvestris* 'Hillside Creeper'). There are many more, but your choice will probably be somewhat limited by availability.

Admittedly, sometimes rapid growers can be pruned slightly each year to maintain an optimum height and width. Many broadleaf evergreens are particularly amenable to an annual trimming. In the countryside surrounding our two story home, *Kalmia latifolia*, the native mountain laurel, grows with abandon. Years ago, I planted several nursery grown specimens in front of our foundation because I wanted the natural look of the area mirrored near our front door. Under ideal conditions, these laurels would have grown 30' tall, but when they topped 6', I cut them back drastically. After a year or two, they filled in nicely as I expected.

Linking the landscape design with the best architectural features of our homes and their surroundings is one of the best ways to achieve harmony of scale and balance. Let's return again to a discussion of how to enhance a few specific house styles.

Victorians:

In a village that I know well, the main street is bordered with a number of historic, carefully maintained Victorian homes. These houses, set back a good distance from the road on broad lawns, are beautifully painted. They are prime examples of that era's highly ornamented style and its gingerbread features, but beneath the front façade of some of them are the usual heavily pruned globes and polygons, conifers that should have been removed years before.

Those who built Victorians from the early 1800s until the last quarter of the century were careful to leave their exteriors free of smothering flora. The last thing that these Victorians wanted to evoke was a reminder of America's forest darkened frontiers. Homeowners of that era thought of their homes as on central stage and built them with many windows to encourage as much sunshine indoors as possible. The comforting front porch, a safe place for children's play and adult relaxation in rockers, is a familiar theme. Unfortunately, there was a drawback—what to do with that high, unattractive area below the porch. This was often trellised and planted with ivy, and that is what remains—which really isn't too bad!

If this trellised area now needs revitalizing while hiding the dead space below the porch, it can be accomplished by planting a row of columnar shaped conifers such as *Taxus baccata* 'Fastigiata', *Thuja occidentalis* 'Emerald' (also called 'Smaragd'), or *Thuja plicata* 'Emerald Cone,' the latter a cultivar of the western arborvitae. The effect is to create a green wall below the house, but these, and many other similar upright conifers, will grow quickly and need constant pruning to maintain their desired height and girth. If you are a Victorian homeowner faced with this common problem, you will probably find the chore less time-consuming than painting all the cutouts, scrolls, and window trim on the house, itself.

Around 1870, these homeowners became enamored of either cottage gardening out front or intricate bedding plant designs. In my opinion, these concepts compete with all the intricate architectural handicraft lavished on the building itself. If you are the owner of a Victorian, why not place the flowering accessories in the rear garden, thus avoiding a busy look to a house that is already well endowed with architectural features?

Better would be to underplant the foundation of the house with a simple evergreen groundcover such as *Vinca minor* or pachysandra (if the area is shady) and possibly, plant-ing a substantial vine on the house corners. This would provide enough detail and allow one's attention to focus on the house itself. Add to this Victorian a broad front lawn, a side framework of a shade tree or two—depending on the space-- and perhaps, a few smaller flowering trees at the corners. Traditionalists should be quite content with such a design.

Cape Cod Cottages:

At the opposite end of the spectrum is the gable-roofed Cape Cod cottage no taller than 1 ½' stories. Allowing tall, out-of-scale shade trees or conifers to dominate such a house reduces the structure to a piddling afterthought. Yet, such landscaping is an exceedingly familiar sight to anyone who has walked or driven around an area filled with these lovely cottages. If yours is a Cape Cod, or any small house for that matter, just imagine how you could regain your dollhouse coziness by eliminating overpowering trees and planting others that are smaller and in-scale.

If I lived in a cottage and liked the appearance of a coniferous tree on my ample front lawn, I would not be content with the ubiquitous Colorado blue spruce. It is too tall, too broad, and too conspicuous to stand in front of a Cape Cod, and I would remove it. Given a reasonably large lawn, I would be more content with the Japanese white pine, *Pinus parviflora glauca*, rather slow growing to an eventual 30', refined, and very picturesque with age. Its blue-green color is a soft, pleasing shade. If I wanted a tall but narrow evergreen tree, I might select *Pinus strobus* 'Fastigiata,' a slender column that, in time, grows 40' tall but to a maximum 10' width.

Or, I might use one of the many slow growing forms of the Serbian spruce, *Picea omorika*, or the oriental spruce, *Picea orientalis*. Of the latter, P.o. 'Gowdy' has short, dark needles and may only reach 10' in height in a decade.

Touches of Americana suit the Cape Cod. Very typical is surrounding the entire front with a white picket fence. But maybe you, like Tom Sawyer, dread the chore of white washing a fence every year. Yet, you like the picket-fence look. Why not cut the job down to a more manageable size by using only two small sections of this fencing in a bed adjacent to the area where drive meets walk ? (a splendid place for a view garden if it can be seen easily from a house window.) While keeping the foundation planting low and simple, use the fence as a backdrop, and use flowering perennials on each side. There is nothing quite like a white fence to set off lovely yellow, pink, or purple flowers, but to avoid an overly fussy appearance, confine the perennials to large groupings of only two or three different varieties. To warm this bed in the winter, you might also add a grouping of dwarf conifers.

Ranch Houses:

A low slung ranch house with a slightly pitched roof is quite another matter. In the truest sense of its usage, the house is meant to hug the earth as though anchored with roots. Continue this perception by planting each corner with an intermediate vertical and, in a slight curve, extend the foundation planting in long, sweeping lines beyond the house corners . Within the sweep, dwarf conifers might look good. Besides the pines mentioned before, low forms of spruce are great—for sunny places. *Picea abies* 'Gnom', with extremely dense needles, is particularly nice. Where a conifer with blue needles would be appropriate, the very low form of the Colorado spruce *Picea pungens* 'St. Mary's Broom' might fit the bill. It is a slow grower with a mounding habit. Many affordable dwarfs will probably be too small to make an immediate impact. This being the case, try filling in temporarily with small evergreen or semi-evergreen azaleas. In time, you can transplant the azaleas elsewhere, an easy task with these fibrous rooted plants. Meanwhile, keep your eye on the conifers to make sure that they have plenty of growing space.

Contemporary Houses:

The low Contemporary or "modern" home with crisp, emphatic lines and sometimes, floor length windows, needs dramatic treatment. Large windows encourage a sunlit interior; yet, many people plant huge specimens so close to the glass that the very light they seek is suppressed. Structural plants usually look very dramatic with this kind of architecture. Some gardeners now find that tall ornamental grasses fit in nicely with contemporary styles. Another possibility, and one that I like very much, is the use of *Yucca filamentosa* (Adam's needle) on each corner of the house. As lone specimens 3-4' tall with 2' long fringed, ribbon-like foliage, and tall spikes of summer flowers, yuccas can be quite interesting. Y. f. 'Golden Sword' is a variegated form with green edges around its yellow centered leaves. Y.f. 'Ivory Tower' is yet another variation, a cultivar that eventually forms large clumps. If you like this look but live in a winter cold zone, you might be surprised to learn that there are also many groundcover succulents that are quite hardy. John Spain, a Connecticut specialist in these plants, grows many forms of opuntia and echinocereus for this use. Some are deciduous but many have evergreen foliage…not just green but gray or gray blue, forest green, and even many tinged with rose. A planting bed of this type can create a futuristic appearance when used at the base of a modern house.

You might repeat this groundcover look at a slight distance in the front of the house but in full view from the house windows. Dwarf or modestly spreading conifers fit well in this kind of view garden. Or, if they do well for you, underplant with one or two kinds of heaths (*Ericas*) or heathers (*Callunas*).

The very tall Contemporary needs a different treatment, particularly more height on each side. Use intermediate spreaders below the windows. On the corners, plant columnar-shaped conifers such as *Juniperus chinensis* 'Robusta Green' or the very slim J.C. 'Spartan.' The later matures at 20' with a width of only 3-4'.

Where a sizeable lawn specimen is desired, a very unusual conifer, especially for an ultramodern home, is the weeping Alaskan cedar, *Chamaecyparis nootkatensis* 'Pendula.' It does, however, require a somewhat moist soil. It's a long name to remember, but as it matures, you'll not soon forget it. In purchasing this cultivar, there may be two slightly different forms, one much narrower than the other, so inquire of a specialist to be certain of its eventual height and width.

Perhaps you are thinking that your house is of an architectural style not mentioned above. In this case, give it a theme that seems suitable to you. Your older home might have one large conifer on the lawn in topnotch condition. You like it very much but it has grown totally out of scale with your front property. Possibly, it can be cut back judiciously, but with such a treasure, I would call in a qualified arborist to do the job.

A few words about pruning conifers: The easiest to control in early spring are yews *(Taxus)*, hemlocks *(Tsuga)*, and Siberian cypress *(Microbiota.)*. Pine *(Pinus)* species can be kept to a reasonable size by clipping off the new candles when they appear. Fir *(Abies)*, cedar, *(Cedrus)*, and Douglas fir *(Pseudotsuga)*, can, if necessary, be pruned back to a bud in spring. Juniper *(Juniperus)*, arborvitae *(Thuja)*, and the false cypress *(Chamaecyparis)*, say the experts, should be pruned only if a stem or two shows reversion to a shape that you had not anticipated. However, pruning off a bit of dead foliage here and there should not do any harm and will immensely improve the appearance of any conifer.

Severing whole branches from conifers can leave unattractive scars, so look carefully backward into the plant before you cut. I, myself, am not a purist, and whenever I see stems that are brown, I clip them off. One of the most common reasons for dead foliage is that a good part of the conifer is being shaded by another plant. If this is your situation, then you may have to do some transplanting.

When revitalizing a planting, determine whether the house, itself, gives you any design clues, something that will give a cohesive look to the whole. An easy clue is the Spanish motif of arched doorways and windows. Try echoing this as an arc in the design of the planting beds. If your entire layout is symmetrical, avoid wavy lines of demarcation for the planting beds. Straight forward geometry is more appropriate here. If your home is a distinct English Tudor, yet English roses are unsightly in the winter, try another kind of high climbing vine over the doorway or at corners. A vine that does very well for me, maybe too well, is *Akebia quinata* with handsome foliage. I have it outside of a greenhouse window where it also shades one corner of our house in summer. Unfortunately, fast growing akebia must be cut back occasionally. Plant it where you want a cover-up. Except in severe climates, akebia is almost evergreen with interesting flowers and fruit, each in season.

For you, the renovating gardener, there is one thing that cannot be stressed too strongly, and that is to space your plants adequately. Now is the time to revitalize your home entrance so that it will remain pleasing long into the future. Spare yourself, and others who come after you, all the work that cramped plantings create. And this means avoiding plants that will all too quickly overgrow their space. Ornamentals pruned heavily to fit a small space remind me of an obese person squeezed into tight clothing, You can easily avoid this look by selecting new plantings that will not need to be corseted with the pruning shears.

CHAPTER VI
MORE OF LESS

CHAPTER VI
More of Less

Longtime gardeners share a pervasive malady; we all love plants too much. Not only is this disease highly infectious, but time exacerbates its hold on us. Often, when we've had great results with one or two species of a single genus, we graduate to the next step—the hot pursuit of collecting every available member of that genus. If we cannot buy it, we propagate it either from seed or cuttings.

More often than not, the most obsessed among us join specialized plant societies. You will find great joy in meeting with others who share your passion for rock garden plants, hostas, conifers, hardy perennials, etc. Unfortunately, and oddly enough, I've never come across a hobby organization that concentrates on studying landscape design.

Observe the gardeners at a plant sale. The rare specimen will always command a steep price even if little is known about it, it is not particularly handsome, or it looks like it might become rampant. Rarity is what gives it value.

I've also noticed that most buyers at a sale tend to purchase only one or two plants of a kind. Visualize these gardeners when they return home trying to decide where best to place their solo acquisitions. This is the reverse of the more satisfactory process—locating a plant or plants that will specifically fit a particular garden space that now looks forlorn and empty. Another thing that I have observed at a plant sale; all the plants already in flower are grabbed up quickly, even if they are not outstanding nor will they be easy to place in the homeowner's garden.

There is no question about it. Avid gardeners tend to be plant collectors. Their reputations are based on the breadth and integrity of their collections. For example, the dedicated rock gardener often covets one-of-a kind gems. His prime objective is to bring many small, magnificent alpines into glorious bloom. Those who display them in troughs often start out by trying to arrange 10, 12, 15 miniatures in a space the size of a kitchen sink. I know because I, too, tend to be this kind of a gardener. Collector gardens, if well done, are places of extreme interest, especially to other specialists. Without a doubt, collecting is great fun, and a most splendid way of studying and appreciating plants at close range--but this is not really landscaping.

Mass Plantings:

It is mass planting that deserves our attention when we are renovating a garden. Mass is what makes the most memorable picture. If you have a large enough garden, perhaps your goal might be to have some areas devoted to a collection and others that use mass as a way of fixing a vivid, unforgettable impression on "that inward eye," as Wordsworth called it. The latter is a lofty goal but well worth achieving.

In spring, it is mass plantings of bulbs that light up the soul of even the most dispassionate of individuals. When planted as a single clump, or even a few clumps, the effect is often that of an afterthought, as though the gardener felt obliged to grow this species somewhere around his house rather than creating a special feature. In selecting bulbs, concentrate on planting as many of the same kind as your space, budget, and energy will allow. That is the kind of thinking that will result in a memorable mass.

In my garden wanderings to near or distant places, I can recall many distinctive specimen plants, but it is the special scene that turns over and over again in my mind. After a visit to the New York Botanical Rock Garden, I came away with a long list of "must try" plants for my garden. Yet, oddly enough, when I think of that amazing place, the first image that pops into my head is that great mass of feathery astilbes along the garden's brook, a common perennial that most people can grow in a damp spot. The curator told us that he tries to create mass wherever possible, and when propagating, produces at least twenty-five plants of the same species. When I'm in a reflective mood, I sometimes call upon my memory to envision such lovely scenes as that great sea of Persian candytuft, *(Aethionema pulchellum)* I observed in a Scottish garden, each plant smothered with rich pink flowers. Or maybe I'll recall that mass of flowering azaleas beside a lake at Callaway Gardens in Georgia or the banks of hydrangeas in a French garden called Le Bois des Moutiers, or the carpet of hardy cyclamen beneath some trees at the Baroness Van Zuylen's Normandy garden. Even closer to home, I think of a shady hillside in Princeton, New Jersey, covered with deep blue *Phlox divaricata* as well as the wonderful drifts of *Primula japonica* at the Leonard J. Buck Garden in Far Hills, New Jersey. Sometimes, it is a combination of two or more beautifully compatible plants that impresses this observer, or maybe it's an outstanding view complimented with a mass planting. While neither you nor I may remember the exact location of some memorable gardens, form, color, and arrangement of an exciting mass planting remains ever fresh in our minds.

One spring day, driving in my own area, I came upon two groupings of six pristine, double white flowering crabapple trees on each side of the entrance to a development. The landscapers could have planted several different varieties, but they repeated the same lovely cultivars, and it made a glorious picture. The drama was repeated later when the crabs came into fruit. This is yet another example of the beauty in planting "en masse."

Monoculture:

Like many another dictum, this one, too, might result in a dilemma. Consider this: repetition of the same species has a name: monoculture. It is an agricultural term that is also used in forestry. Perhaps it is also applicable to any kind of repetitive garden planting. Carried to an extreme, it can be deadly.

To combat this, you should use the utmost discretion and avoid planting the same tree, shrub or perennial in enormous numbers all over your garden. We all know about the demise of two beloved native trees that were once so prevalent here, the American elm and the American chestnut. The former, destroyed by bark beetles, was once a familiar tree planted en masse along many streets in New England. The latter, decimated by an Asiatic fungus, was the most dominant tree in our hardwood forests. When large numbers of the same plant grow in a garden, monoculture, there is always the danger that a new destructive disease or insect will travel quickly from one specimen to the other eventually causing the demise of all. If this happens where there is a mass of one kind of plant in many places throughout the garden, it could cause a serious problem.

Although monoculture sometimes causes problems, nothing is perfect in this world. We should not worry about everything that might occur in the future. What we can do when we grow en masse is to select only those species that are not only attractive but are also known to be relatively disease and insect free at the time they are planted.

Native Plants:

Some say that the answer to this is to grow only native plants. However, this is scarcely the solution since natives are sometimes as subject to natural disasters as introduced plants. How much more American could the elm and chestnut be? And yet, because they existed as a kind of "monoculture" in many areas, their devastating disease and insect attacks traveled from tree to tree wiping out entire populations. Native or introduced, no plant is guaranteed perpetual resistance to the unexpected invasion of a serious malady

Defining the word native, or indigenous, if you prefer that synonym, is a difficult proposition. For example, the genus *Lewisia* is not merely a "native American." It is native to our western mountains. It is not present in the mountains of Eastern United States, nor as far as I know, ever was. Yet, many avid Mid-Atlantic American rock gardeners covet them as native alpine flowers. If they can grow them well here, it is a triumph of expert culture over environmental conditions. Calling the plants "American natives" is not quite accurate.

The geography of the United States is too diverse for this all encompassing label. Then, too, many plants often thought of as natives really originated in places far distant from where we now find them growing wild. The tawny daylily *(Hemerocallis fulva)* of Eastern roadsides, and the yellow flag *(Iris pseudacorus)* of our boggy areas, for example, both originated in Eurasia. The American gardener who feels that he must go "all native" should shun daffodils, tulips, and hyacinths because the original species were indigenous to other countries. What a loss that would be!

Some true natives, such as the clambering fox grape, *Vitis labrusca*, found here by our earliest settlers, became so invasive on our own property that they had to be eliminated even though they were interesting native plants and we enjoyed the taste of their fruits. In our gardens, place your concern with plants that are beginning to spread out of control as were our foxgrapes. The idea of planting all "native" should be replaced with "non-invasive."

I think of the March bank at Winterthur in Delaware which has been called one of our country's finest naturalistic gardens. Slopes of the garden are covered with thousands upon thousands of naturalized bulbs, each variety in its own niche. Almost all are native to other countries, but it is their display en masse that makes them look as though they are the result of a bounteous local Mother Nature.

In many parts of Texas, soils are extremely alkaline. Yet, there are gardeners who grow acidic demanding azaleas from many origins, although they must monitor them carefully and frequently add low PH amendments. Many gardeners in that state are content to grow them merely as annuals. Growing azaleas en masse in this situation is another triumph of expert culture, but for the average Texan, their culture must be frustrating. Compatibility should govern our planting choices.

All the plants that you try to grow, whether native or introduced, can become a maintenance problem or a complete failure unless each readily adapts to the conditions in your garden. If you cultivate many areas, by all means plant "en masse," but also practice diversity of species in as many different places as possible. Unless you are dealing with tender plants, chances are that for a very long time, you will be able to enjoy a splendid--and dramatic--garden. Whenever possible, let's all try to improve our own little paradise with more of less.

CHAPTER VII
MANY SPLENDORED ENDURING COLORS

CHAPTER VII
Many Splendored Enduring Colors

Of all the factors that bring excitement and interest into the garden, probably none creates a more vivid impression than color. If you're the kind of person who enjoys wearing a bright yellow scarf on a neon pink shirt, then you probably have provided bursts of flashy color throughout your garden. There are, of course, garden spaces that benefit from this kind of visual jolt. But more often than not, such an effect just happens, and the gardener who has made it happen is usually unconscious of its effect. This is probably the case with the bright red brick house that I notice every spring. Planted in front of it are magenta flowering azaleas. To me, who prefers more mellow combinations, this is indeed unforgettable—and unpalatable.

When thinking about garden color, flowers usually come first to mind first. Many gardeners are super-sensitive to lovely color combinations, and they spend a great deal of time moving plants around from bed to border and back again until they get the effect that they want. For summer bloom, they might seek out complementary colors by combining such perennials as the yellow *Anthemis tinctoria* 'E.C. Buxton' with the deep purple hues of *Campanula glomerata* 'Superba'. Or, they might have in mind a monochromatic scheme of all yellows featuring *Hemerocallis* 'Hyperion', *Digitalis grandiflora* and *Coreopsis* 'Moonbeam'. The more daring among us might try eye-catching analogous combinations such as the scarlet blooming *Lychnis x arkwrightii* with the orange *Helianthemum* 'Fire Delight', and heat it up even more by adding the bright yellows of *Oenothera missouriensis* that have red buds.

All this is great fun for some gardeners, and it is not surprising that where the dormant season is long, seasonal color is ardently anticipated. I suspect that the most passionate flower lovers in the world live in Alaska or in parts of Canada or in Scandinavia where the brief but heavy bloom period is a highlight of their year.

Most Americans live where the flower season is only six or seven months in length. When it comes to perennials, there might be only a week or two—possibly three or four—when each variety gives its peak performance. Combining perennials, bulbs, and/or annuals creates high drama, but it also requires a lot of thought and some experience to achieve superior results.

Planting deciduous shrubs with outstanding foliage, sometimes variegated, or eye-catching bark or colorful fruit, is another way of evoking further interest, but do you ever think of conifers as colorful? Aren't they, you say, just blobs of green? Not on your life! Mother Nature's evergreen palette, in all its shades and tints, includes a varied selection of foliage colors. Most of us come to appreciate conifers at a more advanced stage of our gardening education. This often coincides with the time when we are in the process of renovating our gardens, and when we do, it hits us like a ton of bricks that conifers can be exceedingly colorful, indeed.

Perhaps you've been thinking: "Ah, yes, our blue Colorado spruce is colorful." Yes, but this massive, ubiquitous conifer, *Picea pungens* 'Glauca', overwhelms many an American lawn as it grows toward its maximum height of 100' sometimes losing many lower branches in the process. Omnipresent in most garden centers and nursery yards, this tree is readily available as a garden transplant. The truth is that few home properties are large enough to support this or many other tall forest trees, and they should be avoided. The conifers that I have in mind are far limited in size making them eminently more suitable for the average home landscaping scheme. When renovating your older garden with ease of maintenance in mind, you might want to consider planting more of these dwarfs. Consider, also, planting slow-growing broadleafs and/or low deciduous shrubs with unusually colorful foliage.

Some years ago, as I worked at designing and supervising the plantings of private suburban gardens, I became aware of the many dwarf conifers with unusual forms, textures, and foliage that were beginning to enter the marketplace. At that time, the landscaping public was not quite aware of their value and, as a whole, was not ready to pay a steep price for the unfamiliar. I tried to grow what I could in my own small nursery, but even obtaining good stock was sometimes a problem. Nurserymen in the far West and Europe, I might add, were way ahead of those in the Northeast in growing and selling these plants.

Happily, this situation no longer exists, and if you seek out dwarf conifers, many can now be located at local nurseries. You will find them with foliage in a variety of tints, tones, and tinges. For the truly uncommon types, mail order is also a possible resource, but be prepared. The cost of shipping is so high that you will probably have to buy these plants in a small size. I solved this problem for myself by buying small and growing them on until they have a bit of presence. All you need is an out-of-the-way, temporary nursery area. Good gardeners are patient gardeners.

Let us take a closer look at conifers. Many, like the average yew, have foliage that is a deep, dark green. Yet, there are many "aurea" forms that are distinctively golden. Some conifers array themselves in hues of gray-blue or silver. And then, too, you can find many variegated forms with yellow or white tips; still others have highlights of silver, like the streaks in a matron's graying hair. However, be forewarned. Using these colorful cultivars to best advantage requires subtle judgment--unless you want to create a planting as gaudy as a Spanish dancer. A little goes a long way.

What we sometimes forget is that on every residential property, other than the sky above, the lawn below, and the few tall trees that you probably have already if yours is an older garden, the greatest block of color is the house itself. Using the front of your home as an effective backdrop for color coordinating with foliage can produce magical results. In garden areas more distant from the house, you can continue this effect by matching plants with the color of a detached garage, fence, arbor, or even a storage shed.

Some time ago, I chanced upon a little book called "Old House Colors" by Lawrence Schwinn III. In it, I discovered that down through the ages, traditionalists painted their houses and trim with specific colors which were illustrated in this book. To be in keeping with their age and style, certain color combinations were deemed "by the experts" proper and suitable. All this seems rather arbitrary in our age which prides itself on free and imaginative expression. But this is what we can do when renovating our gardens: using our homes as a backdrop, color coordinate the building with the tones and shades of our plants. Color contributes to character. Some colors convey excitement—bright yellow, for example. Others, such as gray-blue or silver, convey the sensation of peace, tranquility, sophistication. You might also grow plants with distinctive flowers or foliage in an out-of-the-way garden for the specific purpose of providing cutting material to coordinate with an indoor room. If the plant that you admire simply does not fit in with your overall garden scheme, growing it strictly for cutting material might be the way to go.

Each of us carries our own prejudices about what is pleasing and what is discordant. For me, I feel that a charming old house solidly built of stone should never be completely covered with plants. Let the pleasing colors and textures of the stone, or merely a facade of stone, provide most of the color and texture rather than leaving this only to clambering vines. After planting vines, keep a watchful eye on their growth, pruning them heavily, if necessary, so that a good portion of the stone is always visible.

The front of such a house needs a simple planting scheme. Certainly, deep green conifers or broadleafs can look appealing; variegated plants are best avoided because they will steal from the beauty of the stones.

Brick is a little different in character. Whether it is smooth or corrugated, the landscape designer can be a little more daring with color choices. I especially like the cheerful effect of white trim added to a red brick house. If this describes your home, you might set it off by introducing the new pyramidal Japanese black pine, *Pinus thunbergii* 'Thunderhead' at your house corners. The pine is an intermediate, which means that it probably will not exceed 6' in ten years. Its outstanding feature is that both its winter buds and spring candles are white in color, unusual for any pine. How nicely it repeats the white on the house; "a color echo" as some authors call it.

The white house with red trim, especially if it has a path of red brick, can be a little more generous in its repetition of this bright color. Perhaps it is best to plant a dark green conifer such as *Taxus baccata procumbens*, foliage the color of a cucumber, in front of the house, but you can repeat the red trim at the house corners (if plenty of space is available) with the branches of a red-stemmed dogwood shrub, *Cornus sericea*. With ample room, a grouping of these shrubs would be even better. Compact forms of the deciduous dwarf variety 'Kelseyi' are available with a little searching.

You could also try planting the broadleaf andromeda *Pieris japonica* 'Mountain Fire' near this house. Its emerging growth is bright red, its foliage dark green, early spring flowers white, and it reputedly does well in sun as well as light shade.

Another way to carry over the red theme is the use of the native deciduous holly called winterberry *(Ilex verticillata)* in one of its many cultivars. It grows well in wet soils. Native on our property, winterberries will also do well in moderately dry soils. Their summer foliage is dark green, but they are real standouts in fall and winter with their brilliant red fruit.

When dealing with verticillata hollies, the one thing to remember is to grow a pollinating male within a reasonable distance of the female. The only sure way of locating both sexes is by visiting a nursery that sells these hollies in late autumn, and you'll see for yourself the fruiting females and non-fruiting males. Labels on this species, I've found, can be very misleading. Imagine my surprise when the 'Rhett Butler' verticillata I had just purchased turned out to be the female 'Scarlet O'Hara'!

If your house is high enough, you might want to plant the corners with the evergreen holly *Ilex x aquiperni* 'San Jose' Its conical shape is, by no means, a dwarf, as it can grow to more than 20' tall, but the fruits, a deep red, are most abundant and showy.

Several groundcover plants also carry through with the red theme. Try combining hollies with the red foliaged groundcover *Sedum spurium* 'Fuldaglut', which is red all season rather than the more commonly used S. s. 'Dragon's Blood.' Where it is hardy, the ornamental grass, *Imperata* 'Red Baron', is another possibility. Yet another is the partially evergreen *Bergenia* x 'Evening Glow', a new introduction, with red flowers in spring and bronze foliage, but the leaves of this species do get a little ragged in a Zone 5 winter. Only recently, I planted a grouping of wintergreens *(Gaultheria procumbens)* for a friend. I thought that gaultherias are quite finicky needing just the right amount of sun and just the right amount of shade, but we decided to give them a try. We must have found the right spot because the wintergreens are doing well on the north side of the house where the soil has been made more acidic with peat moss amendments. These low evergreen clumps bear rather large dark red fruits, an exceedingly attractive combination near a brick red house.

Many shrubs, such as cotoneasters, hawthorns, and crabapples have deep red winter fruit, including the firethorn *(Pyracantha coccinea)*. But if the color you are after is red, and not orange, you had better select the variety with great care.

If your house (or outbuilding) is red, white, or gray, the bark of a clump of the Japanese silver birch, *Betula platyphyllum* 'Whitespire' will add a beautiful chalky white accent to your scheme. Pruned high enough, the white of the bark will be a focal point throughout the seasons. This birch has shown resistance to the often disfiguring birch leaf borer; there are a few other white birches that are also relatively insect free.

Imagine, if you will, a ranch house painted slate blue or some shade of gray. Possibly it has never been painted at all but has weathered a silvery gray. If you are reworking your foundation planting, and you like a refined monochromatic scheme as much as I do, then you might plant the house corners with the columnar shaped spruce *Picea glauca* 'Sander's Blue' with green-blue foliage. Or, if you can locate it, try *Pinus koraiensis* 'Morris Blue' for this position. The later, however, is rather fast growing and will achieve a height of 10' and a width of 5' in about ten years. In front of the house, low mounds of *Juniperus squamata* 'Blue Star' might be right for their deep, silvery blue effect. Another possibility for under low windows is *Juniperus sabina* 'Blue Forest'. When it fills out in width, it looks like an enchanted, hoary forest.

One of the conifers that I like is the true silver-blue *Picea pungens* 'R.H. Montgomery', a blue spruce cultivar that is far more interesting—and size limited--than the species. This slow-growing plant has a horizontal shape, but it can eventually reach a height of 5'. The Montgomery might look truly elegant near a pale gray house.

A great opportunity for animated color combinations occurs when the house is a pale yellow brick, or if frame, painted butter yellow or mustard gold, or even white with yellow trim. That is because there is a wide variety of dwarf conifers with golden needles or gold colored highlights. Those that will do well with an eastern, western, or southern exposure are cultivars of the false hinoki cypress *(Chamaecyparis obtusa)* and the sawara cypress *(Chamaecyparis pisifera)*.

For a vertical specimen at the corner of a very low house (or as an accent in a "view garden), try the slow growing C.o. 'Nana Aurea' , which will probably reach 20" in height, but only a foot in width at the end of ten years. Another vertical along these lines is the slow growing C. o.'Nana Lutea' which changes with the seasons from a pure gold to foliage with a white and gold tint. 'C. o. 'Crippsii' is yet another golden pyramid. This one grows far too large to work with any but the most massive house. It is probably better for use at a distance. If your winters are usually severe, it might get a little freezer burn, but that be trimmed away.

Horizontal yellow forms are just as numerous. C.o. 'Gold Spangles' is a deep gold color that grows 20" tall and 3' wide. One expert recommends that it be sheared slightly each spring to maintain its dense habit. Then there is the handsome C.o. 'Pygmea Aurescens'. Unfortunately, this conifer's color can be as somewhat fickle. It has a yellow copper sheen in winter which becomes a brighter yellow in spring, and then, again, chartreuse in summer.

Another golden shrub that I particularly like is the spreading English yew, *Taxus baccata* 'Repandens Aurea'. The plant that I observed was a low mound 3' across and about 2' tall, but in time, it will probably grow into a very broad specimen.

If you wish to color coordinate a groundcover under one of these conifers or by itself against the foundation of a yellow house or a white house with yellow trim, you might try the new variegated *Vinca minor* 'Illumination'. This myrtle, yellow in leaf and edged with green, will spread beneath taller plants in either sun or shade. A grouping of three to five of the variegated types set amid the green species might be just the right touch.

Some conifers with golden foliage look positively jaundiced in winter, and I will have none of them. One of these is *Pinus mugo* 'Aurea'. Before purchasing conifers with an unusual color, it's a good idea to inspect them in a botanical garden or specialty nursery—in winter--and then judge for yourself. Another thing to keep in mind is to use plant color sparingly. One truly yellow specimen may be more than enough in a small foundation planting along with solid green specimens.

For a yellow accent that is a little more subtle, don't overlook shrubs that bear golden yellow fruit in fall and winter. The compact and charming Japanese holly *Ilex crenata* 'Yellow Fruit' might be just the ticket. It has tiny evergreen leaves and is hardy to at least Zone 6. For fruiting, both male and female specimens are needed.

A white house with pink trim, delicate and dainty, speaking of old lace and finely polished indoor furniture, is easy to color-coordinate with summer flowers, but winter interest is far more difficult to achieve. One possibility might be to use the 10' tall spruce *Picea abies* 'Acrocona ' on a house corner. It is said to bear many raspberry pink cones. An unusual feature of this plant, so I have read, is that these cones appear mostly on the tips of the branches. Another upright possibility here is the use of *Pieris japonica* 'Valley Valentine' with maroon buds and rose-pink blooms in spring.

The beige, tan, or brown house, painted or stained to have an earthy feeling, might be best color coordinated with foliage colors of pure green, bronze, or copper. *Mahonia aquifolium*, the Oregon grape holly, is a favorite shrub of mine because its leaves are so lustrously bronze all winter in a slightly protected spot. However, except for M. repens, which I grow beneath semi-evergreen azaleas for wind protection, the genus is not hardy enough here in Zone 5, and looks shabby after a tough winter. Then, too, it never produces yellow flowers here, nor the grapelike fruit of autumn. There is a compact form growing to 30" in height called M. a. 'Mayhan Strain' which might be of tougher mettle.

The heaths *(Erica)* and heathers *(Calluna)* also bite the dust whenever I plant them in my climate. Hopefully, you have had better luck. Of them, the spring heath, *Erica carnea*, seems to be the hardier of the two. If I were looking for a groundcover with salmon-copper foliage, I'd surely try *Erica carnea* 'Sherwoodii', but it probably needs some winter protection north of Virginia.

To cascade over a wall near the brown-beige house, my choice would be *Cotoneaster dammeri* 'Coral Beauty" with fruits distinctly orange in color. Nursery catalogues usually list the color as "red," but orange, I think, best describes them.

All these suggestions are merely meant to stimulate your thinking about distinctive color combinations. There are, of course, many more plants that might be suitable, but my purpose here is to sharpen your awareness of the possibilities. If, however, your prime goal as landscaper is to create a naturalistic garden, realize that during the growing season, plants with unusual foliage colors are an anomaly not often created by Mother Nature. In such a garden, shades of greens might be more suitable. Go especially easy with the bright yellows.

If you like the idea of coordination but you have already decided on "must-have" replacement plants that would look discordant with the color of your house, then a spade may not be your first tool of action. It is probably time to get out the paintbrush instead and coat your wooden structures to fit your plant selections. But don't stop there. You might follow through by also painting your shed, garage, or porch. If you should be fortunate enough to have a feature such as an arbor or pergola, paint that, too—the same color.

PHOTO ALBUM
Removals

TOP:

PREPARATION FOR RENOVATING AN OLDER GARDEN AREA USUALLY BEGINS WITH REMOVAL.

BOTTOM:

A SMALL TRACTOR AND CART FOR COLLECTING REMOVALS ARE LABOR SAVING EQUIPMENT.

Patios

TOP:

BRICK PAVERS WERE USED FOR THEIR POOL-SIDE PATIO BY DRS. HELGA & REINHARD SCHWARTZ

BOTTOM:

IN MID-MAY, BLOOMING DELAWARE VALLEY AZALEAS ARE A PLEASING CONTRAST

TO THE BLUESTONES OF THE PATIO.

FLOWERING CREEPERS ARE INTERSPERSED AMONG THE BLUESTONE FLAGS IN THE GARDEN OF SUSAN DEEKS.

CLEAN, CLEAR RUN-AWAY SPRING WATER WAS TEMPORARILY IMPOUNDED TO FORM A LITTLE COUNTRY POND.

TOP:

A SECOND STORY DECK OVERLOOKS A BRIDGE CROSSING THE BROOK,

A ROCK GARDEN, AND THE MEADOW GARDEN.

BOTTOM:

THIS SCENE, IN THE GARDEN OF JIM AVENS, IS OFTEN ENJOYED FROM AN INDOOR SUNROOM.

Change of Elevation

TOP:

A DRY-LAID WALL OF LOCAL STONE SEPARATES TWO PARTS OF THE GARDEN AND INVITES THE CURIOUS TO MOVE ON TO THE UPPER LEVEL.

BOTTOM:

FOR SAFETY'S SAKE, THESE PICTURESQUE, THOUGH ROTTING RAILROAD TIE STEPS, HAD TO BE REPLACED.

TOP:

LOG AND GRAVEL STEPS CLIMB THE REAR OF HELEN AND FRANK DONN'S WATNONG GARDEN.

BOTTOM:

THIN SLATE SLABS ACCENT THE STAIRCASE OF LIMESTONE AND SANDSTONE BLOCKS IN IRELAND'S

GLASNEVIN BOTANICAL GARDEN

Dwarf Conifers

TOP:

LOW, SLOW GROWING CONIFERS ALONG A FRONT PATH PROVIDE ALL-YEAR INTEREST.

BOTTOM:

THE DONN'S GARDEN FEATURES PRIZED DWARF CONIFERS.

CAREFULLY SELECTED LIMESTONE BOULDERS AND DWARF CONIFERS
(SUCH AS THE GOLDEN-TIPPED *Thuja plicata* 'CUPREA' IN THE CENTER)
ARE THE PRIME FEATURES OF THIS GARDEN CREATED BY HOMEOWNER IRVING WINTER.

Paths

TOP:

WEDGE-SHAPED DECKING ON WET GROUND BENDS THE REAR PATH TOWARDS THE HOUSE DOOR.

BOTTOM:

A STEP UP (OR DOWN) ON THIS PATH CLIMBS THE SLIGHT SLOPE.

Perennials

TOP:

ALONG THE DRIVEWAY, PERENNIALS AUGMENT THE FLOWERING CRABAPPLES IN MAY.

BOTTOM:

THE RED AND WHITE SUMMER MEADOW GARDEN FEATURES A BACKDROP OF

THE CANADIAN WEIGELA 'RED PRINCE'.

TOP:

HOSTAS OF ALL SIZES AND SHAPES ARE PERFECT FOR SHADY GARDENS.

BOTTOM:

THE PASTEL COLORED BLOOMS OF SOME PERENNIALS SOFTEN A WARM DAY IN JUNE.

Crowding

TOP:

LOW, LUSH AZALEA 'CORSAGE', NOW ENCROACHING ON THE PATH, GREW 9' IN WIDTH IN 30 YEARS.

BOTTOM:

AZALEA 'TRADITION' IS SWAMPED BY FADING DAFFODIL FOLIAGE AND EVER-ENLARGING HOSTAS.

Fencing

TOP:

HOMEOWNER CONSTRUCTED BOARD SLAT FENCING AT WATNONG GARDENS

PROVIDES BOTH PRIVACY AND GOOD AIR CIRCULATION.

BOTTOM LEFT:

THIS FENCING OF HORIZONTAL WOOD SLATS WAS CONSTRUCTED BY THE HOMEOWNER FOR HIS MEADOW GARDEN.

BOTTOM RIGHT:

A FENCE OF CLOSE-BOARD PICKETS REPELS DEER IN THE GARDEN OF JIM AVENS.

Gates

TOP:

THIS AUTOMATIC GATE IS CONNECTED TO HEAVY GAUGE POLYPROPYLENE FENCING TO DETER DEER.

BOTTOM:

THIS MEADOW GATE, WHERE WATER TENDS TO GATHER, IS ACCENTED WITH A SPECIMEN

VARIEGATED JAPANESE WILLOW.

TOP:

THIS GATE WAS PURCHASED AT A RUMMAGE SALE!

IT IS ACCENTED WITH A HARP, GREEN IRELAND'S NATIONAL SYMBOL.

BOTTOM:

A FRENCH STYLE LATTICE GATE, GARDEN OF MOLLY HUDSON, IS FRAMED WITH A CLIMBING WHITE WISTERIA.

Benches

TOP:

A BENCH IN THE STYLE OF SIR EDWIN LUTYENS, AN EARLY 20TH CENTURY ARCHITECT,

NICELY COMPLIMENTS THE ROCK WALL BEHIND IT AT MORRIS ARBORETUM.

BOTTOM:

A SIMPLE CONCRETE BENCH ADDS CHARM TO THIS SCENE AT THE MCGOURTY'S

HILLSIDE GARDEN IN CONNECTICUT.

TOP:

WHERE MANY PEOPLE GATHER, AN OVERSIZED BENCH IS NEEDED AS HERE AT THE MORIKAMI IN FLORIDA.

BOTTOM:

SIMPLY DESIGNED CHAIRS AND BENCHES OVERLOOK A SPRING GARDEN IN PRINCETON, NEW JERSEY.

Garden Objet d'Art

AN OVER-TURNED JUG IS THE FOCAL POINT AMIDST THE PLANTINGS IN THIS GARDEN IN FRANCE.

Gazebos

TOP:

A GAZEBO, OR SUMMER HOUSE AS IT IS SOMETIMES CALLED,

IS A SPECIAL FEATURE OF THE ROBERTSON'S GARDEN ON NORTH ISLAND, NEW ZEALAND.

BOTTOM:

THIS GAZEBO, IN A PRINCETON, NEW JERSEY GARDEN,

IS A FAVORITE SPOT FOR ENTERTAINING ON A HOT SUMMER DAY.

Water

TOP:

Iris pseudacorus, IN SHALLOW WATER, ADDS JUNE COLOR TO THE EDGES OF A COUNTRY POND

BOTTOM:

THIS POOL WAS DUG FROM AND EDGED WITH LAVA ROCK IN THE COUNTRY OF NEW ZEALAND.

THE HOUSE AT FROG POND FARM IS REFLECTED IN STILL WATERS.

Terraced Walls

TOP:

RAILROAD TIE WALLS AND CASCADING AZALEAS BLEND WELL WITH THE HEAVY WOODLAND

BEHIND IT IN A NATURALISTIC GARDEN.

BOTTOM:

A BEAUTIFULLY CONSTRUCTED BRICK WALL ENCLOSES THE PATIO IN SUSAN DEEK'S GARDEN.

Rock Walls

TOP:

THE ROCK FOUNDATION OF AN OLD BARN IN ITHACA, NY SERVES AS THE BACKDROP FOR A SPLENDID

PERENNIAL GARDEN. THE HOMEOWNER-DESIGNER IS LANDSCAPE ARCHITECT PETER TROWBRIDGE.

BOTTOM:

ROCK, COLLECTED FROM THE ROADSIDES BY THE HOMEOWNERS,

WAS USED FOR CONSTRUCTING THESE DRY-LAID TERRACED WALLS.

Rock Gardens

TOP:

THIS RAISED BED, FILLED WITH GRAVELLY SOIL, MAKES IT POSSIBLE

TO GROW ALPINE-TYPE PLANTS IN NORTHERN NEW JERSEY.

BOTTOM:

A BACKDROP OF MID-SEASON AZALEAS FRAMES THIS SAME ROCK GARDEN.

TOP:

SPECIES DIANTHUS FLOURISHES IN THIS WELL-DRAINED SOIL.

BOTTOM:

A FEW LOW SHRUBS, SUCH AS *Spiraea bumalda* 'CRISPA', GIVE SUMMER COLOR TO THIS ROCK GARDEN.

Driveways

A NEW ZEALAND HOMEOWNER CONSTRUCTED COBBLESTONE DRIVEWAY

NICELY FITS IN WITH ITS SURROUNDING ROCK GARDENS

Color Coordination

TOP:

THE BURGUNDY TRIM OF THIS HOUSE AND GARAGE IS COLOR-COORDINATED WITH A JAPANESE MAPLE,

THE BARBERRY 'CRIMSON PYGMY' AND AUTUMN FLOWERING SEDUMS.

BOTTOM:

ANNUALS COORDINATE WITH THE COLORS OF THE BRICK PATH

IN THE GARDEN OF SALLY AND CONNIE KALLAS.

Groundcovers

TOP:

AN ENCLOSED BED OF MYRTLE, WITH A STEPPING STONE IN THE CENTER,

IS A SURE-PROOF WAY OF EDGING A WALK.

BOTTOM:

RIPRAPPING, AS HERE AT THE MORIKAMI IN FLORIDA, IS BUT ONE WAY OF TREATING

PART A DIFFICULT-TO-MOW LAWN OR WATER'S EDGE.

XXIX

Exceptional Shrubs

TOP:

DAPHNE X BURKWOODII 'SOMERSET' IS A LOW SHRUB PRIZED FOR ITS EARLY BLOOM.

BOTTOM:

THESE AZALEAS, THE CULTIVAR 'GREETING', PROVIDE DRAMATIC

SEASONAL COLOR IN THE NORTH SIDE OF THE PATIO.

TOP:

VIBURNUM PLICATUM 'WATANABEI' BLOOMS ON AND OFF ALL SEASON

BOTTOM:

THE OAKLEAF HYDRANGEA BRINGS MID-SEASON BLOOMS TO SHADY PARTS OF THE GARDEN.

TOP:

AZALEA 'HERBERT' AND *Rhododendron* 'JANET BLAIR' HAVE FINE FOLIAGE

AND EXTRAORDINARY BLOOM POWER

BOTTOM:

HERE IS A SELECTION OF THE MOUNTAIN LAUREL

(*Kalmia latifolia* 'SARAH') WITH RED BLOOMS FOLLOWING RED BUDS.

Exceptional Trees

TOP:

Prunus 'WAYSIDE WEEPING WHITE' IS THE EARLIEST TREE TO BLOOM AT FROG POND FARM.

BOTTOM LEFT:

Acer palmatum 'BLOODGOOD' AND THE DWARF *A.p. dissectum* 'CRIMSON QUEEN'
ARE TWO OF MANY ELEGANT JAPANESE MAPLES.

BOTTOM RIGHT: *Cornus kousa*, THE KOREAN DOGWOOD, OFTEN BLOOMS FOR AT LEAST TWO MONTHS.

Wildflowers

TOP:

BLOODROOT, A LOVELY EARLY SPRING WILDFLOWER, IS SHOWN HERE IN ITS RARE,

BUT INCREDIBLY DOUBLE FORM.

BOTTOM:

HANDS-OFF WHEN THE SELF-SOWN NATIVE WEED, JOE-PYE, APPEARS.

THIS BEAUTIFUL ASCLEPIAS SPECIES IS A TREASURED PERENNIAL IN EUROPE.

Early and Late Autumn And Winter

AN EARLY NOVEMBER SNOWFALL BLANKETS THE GRASS

BEFORE THIS JAPANESE MAPLE LOSES ITS DECIDUOUS FOLIAGE.

TOP:

SWEETGUM TREES FORM A COLORFUL AUTUMN BACKDROP TO THE MEADOW GARDEN.

BOTTOM:

HEAVY SNOW OFTEN COVERS THIS GARDEN FOR MOST OF THE WINTER.

Deer

WELCOME, WHITE TAILED DEER!

AT LEAST, THESE THREE ARE WELCOME ADDITIONS IN THE DALLAS, TEXAS BOTANICAL GARDEN.

THEY ARE BRONZE STATUES.

CHAPTER VIII

LOWER MAINTENANCE RAISES GARDEN PLEASURE

CHAPTER VIII.
Lower Maintenance Raises Garden Pleasure

You won't enjoy the beauty that lurks in every corner of your property if you are worn to a frazzle trying to maintain it. There is quite a difference between being frazzled and developing a sensible garden routine. By reorganizing and eliminating some of your repetitive but non-productive garden tasks, that plot of land that you tend will become pure pleasure and not pure pain.

In my own country area, jogging is a favorite form of exercise. Once I read a study that said: in women over 50, gardening is far better than jogging for increasing bone density and avoiding osteoporosis. Reading no further, I once again grabbed a cultivator and a trowel and cleaned out a bed of weeds. Gardening, apparently, is as good for the body as it is for the soul although I did not need any excuse for engaging in an activity that produces so much of interest so close at hand.

Gardeners who sometimes shuffle from one obsessive garden project to another, often get off track through the years and forget to keep in mind the whole design picture. In doing so, many repetitive tasks might become necessary that could now be eliminated. Let's take a look at some of the basic parts of your total picture with lower maintenance in mind. Use your site plan if you've worked one out. If you feel intimidated by the task of drawing up such a plan (as explained in Chapter III) because it simply is not be your cup of tea, consider engaging a landscape designer to prepare one for you. A talented designer may be able to shed light on some of your stickiest, most time consuming projects-- and possibly save you money to boot.

1. Establish A Theme:

A garden is merely a collection of unrelated parts if it does not have a basic theme. Like a meandering brook, a theme should appear as only a trickle in places and in full flood elsewhere. For example, if you love the look of a cottage garden or any informal arrangement of flowering plants, let it appear in full flood in one prominent place, but return to it elsewhere in small doses. Let it sing out as the distinctive signature by which your garden is known. Other areas of sharp contrast can create interest, but a recapitulation of the original theme satisfies the human need for returning to the familiar.

2. Secondary Themes:

Few long-time gardeners will be content with only one theme, especially if they are horticulturally minded; secondary themes are sometimes needed to sustain interest throughout the property. If this describes your needs, and you cultivate a conifer area or perennial borders or a rock garden or an extensive patch of wildflowers, then these secondary themes might already be in place. Or perhaps you are now considering adding a new theme or two but are afraid that it will require too much maintenance. Here's how to make your decision:

First, locate the secondary theme on your plan and see whether it looks awkward or natural in the place you've chosen. If the latter, then consider how easily you can supply that location with special soil mixes and/or mulches, whether you must constantly buy or propagate the needed plants, whether the area is a reasonable distance from an irrigation outlet, etc. No amount of effort is too much if you are certain that this project is something that really inspires you, but realize that a garden, like a child, does not thrive on neglect, and you must have the time to devote to it.

Before you plan on renovating or creating a structural feature such as a gazebo, an arbor, or a pergola, consider how much or how little use it will receive. Covered with vines, furnished with benches, each can be a pleasantly shady place to sit and drink iced tea on a hot summer day. Bring out the cold beer if you prefer, but when refreshments from the kitchen are at a great distance, this walk might require a balancing act that you do not want to repeat too often. Before restoration or construction, think it out carefully to be certain that the structure is worth the effort and the expense.

When well built, one or all of the above can be delightful focal points. But be practical. If you have an arbor that supports climbing roses that never seem to do very well, or if the arbor requires painting all too often or shows signs of rot, then removing it may be no loss at all. In the older garden, subtraction is often far more important than addition.

I think of the small 15" deep ornamental pool in our natural stream that was a pleasing feature here for many years. However, in time, silt from the stream clogged up the pool and frequently had to be removed--by hand. Eventually, we gave up on the pool and converted it into a shallow basin covered with watercress. Finding an alternate, less time consuming use for an existing feature is sometimes possible.

Perhaps you have decided that what you really would like to have is a rock garden of precious alpines. This can be a superbly interesting project, but realize that the majority of these plants are at their prime from early spring to midsummer. If the place you've selected is off your patio, and you seldom use your patio before high summer, you might prefer looking out at an extravagant display of annuals or perennials at that time of the year. Think it all through before you commit to your plan. Combine use of site in a way that will fulfill your needs and desires for each month of the outdoor year.

If you want to incorporate a special feature in the future but, at present, it is beyond your budget, then add it to your site plan. When you are eventually able to develop that feature, getting to it might mean destroying a temporary area that you've created in the meantime. Double work! Instead, leave that space simple and open until you're ready for the permanent project.

Sometimes, you can anticipate a future necessity. If, for example, you expect to replace your underground oil tank, it will certainly require heavy equipment to remove the old and install the new. Spending too much time now on an area that will be inevitably uprooted is wasted effort.

3. Outdoor Dining:

Whether you call your paved area a patio or terrace (they are basically the same), it will be as useful as a broom without a handle if its location is an uncomfortable distance from your kitchen. No amount of beautification will increase your enjoyment of the patio if it is not handy. Of course, there is always the possibility of creating a food preparation area within the confines of a distant patio if you have a large family or if you plan to entertain outdoors many times each summer.

Another factor in the usefulness of a patio is the condition of its paving. If paving stones are loose or cracked in places (very common if they are older than twenty years) you might find yourself either avoiding the area or fussing with it frequently to achieve a temporary solution, a high maintenance task if ever there was one. This sometimes happens when an old brick patio is paved with soft, rather than cold weather tolerant brick. Cracking and scaling can be so severe that the bricks really must be replaced. Recycle the old bricks, if you can, by using them in a protected area. (I used discarded bricks at the bottom of my cold frame)! Replacing a patio is a major proposition but the sooner you get to it, the sooner you will be able to enjoy dining outdoors on pleasant summer evenings.

Let us suppose that your present patio is a cracked concrete slab that you abhor. Yet, you dread the heavy labor of tearing it up and disposing of the materials. You could have it repoured by contractors, this time mixing a pebbled aggregate into the surface for a more natural look. This is not a "handy man's special" kind of a job. You will have to find an artistic contractor who is experienced in this kind of work.

If you strive to keep your garden as natural as possible, then you might choose to have a patio consisting of irregular flagstones set in sand. Crazy paving is what the British call rough-cut fieldstone which comes in a variety of shapes set with the joints running off in all directions. If this is the look that intrigues you, then your patio probably fits the informal character of the rest of your garden. You will need to weed between the cracks on a regular basis. If you choose to do so, you can plant the cracks with creeping thyme or one of many flat, flowering, mat-like species which offer beauty and fragrance. In time, such a planting will reduce your weeding chores.

On the other hand, perhaps your present patio paving is satisfactory but the exposure is not ideal. Do you find yourself reaching for sunglasses as you dine because the setting sun is always in your eyes when you sit down for the evening meal? You would like to expand the space slightly into a shady corner but without making it a large project. If your patio was constructed with materials that can no longer be easily matched, the project becomes problematic. A possible solution is to add an entirely different section of flooring to your present area, perhaps a platform of wooden decking on which the dining table can be set.

If the patio's size is skimpy and/or much of the material needs replacement, think about tearing it out and starting anew. Begin by drawing it on paper, especially if a new location is what you want. Situate it in a place that is both convenient and, if possible, protected from heavy windstorms. An alcove between two sections of the house is often a superior site. Whatever the possibilities, be sure that the area is large enough for the table, chairs, barbecue, and the number of people that you'll want to entertain. Keep in mind that outdoor furniture takes up much more room than indoor furniture. As with a home greenhouse, the space provided is often too small.

If the cost of traditional patio flooring, such as brick, is beyond what you are able to spend, you might consider installing dry laid interlocking concrete pavers. In my opinion, they look better as flooring than when used for retaining walls. The pavers are now available in rounds and rectangles in a variety of sizes, and the choice in colors and textures is so broad that almost any desired effect can be simulated. The trick in designing is to refine your choices so that they blend in with the surroundings as well as fit your budget. Limit your pavers to one or two patterns because it is serenity you are trying to create, not the busy intricacy of a patchwork quilt.

A dry-laid patio (one constructed without mortar) needs sand and/or rock dust or grit in the excavated area to support the paving stones. These materials will permit water to penetrate easily below the paving rather than to sit above in puddles. From my own experience, I prefer to see builder's sand used at the base with rock dust or grit near the surface. Sand used throughout has a tendency to creep to the surface and eventually, requires a great deal of sweeping. This is one maintenance headache that can steal time from the busy groundskeeper. Remember, you are striving for low maintenance!

The basic steps involved in constructing a dry-laid patio are as follows:

1. Excavate a sub-base 3 to 8", the deeper measurement if your area is subject to substantial frost each winter. Below the finished grade of the patio, place sand topped with rock dust or grit. Firm with a heavy-duty tamper. Check frequently with a tape measure to maintain an even depth, and fill in further with rock dust or grit where necessary.

2. Before setting pavers, apply a geotextile fabric to inhibit weed growth.

3. Insure an even height with the use of a leveling board

4. Install edging materials (see below).

5. Set pavers as close together as possible. If some of the pavers must be cut to conform to a pattern, you might want to rent a brick saw to do the job.

6. Go over the entire finished surface with the rock dust filling in any gaps between the pavers. Tamp the surface in two directions.

An outline edging material will be needed to keep the materials in place, and this should be installed as soon as possible. Many homeowners construct a low wall with materials that are compatible to the flooring. This creates a nice place for auxiliary seating and/or for displaying interesting container plants. Another common edging material is pressure treated lumber or railroad ties sunk into the ground about 4" deep. However, if your patio outline is curved, it is impossible to bend this wood. Instead, you might use six inch deep heavy duty black vinyl edging. I think it is preferable to metal edging because it has no sharp edges, and if anchored properly with tapered steel stakes, should prove to be more or less permanent. Bricks also make a nice edging, especially if they are used elsewhere on the house or grounds. They can be set diagonally or even arranged in a double tier for large patios.

Good sized boulders can sometimes be used as corner stones, but it might be necessary to cement these rocks in place so that the patio blocks and grit will be well contained. Choose boulders with a flat upper surface if you can find them. They'll do double duty as temporary seating.

Surrounding every inch of the typical patio with flower beds is not, to my way of thinking, always a good idea. It imposes an artificial look to the area, something I try to avoid whenever possible. Perhaps one bed, or possibly two to round a corner, will be more than enough. Then, too, a patio is the perfect place to display some of those tender container plants that might look lost in the garden, itself.

The considerations I've outlined above are meant to be merely a primer on what you will encounter when embarking on such a project, but before you begin--especially if you plan on doing the work yourself--thoroughly research the construction methods that are involved. Those who market paving blocks usually provide plenty of information. All work will require good access to the site. A cart pulled by a small tractor is easier to manage than a hand-pushed wheelbarrow. You will need a place as close to the construction site as possible to store your materials. If you have never before tackled so large a project, then you might want to do a trial project in a small area such as the base for a birdbath. Don't underplay the perseverance that a large project will demand -- what one might call "true grit."

The cost factor may, in the long run, dictate your choice of materials. Repouring concrete will probably be less expensive than starting from scratch with traditional materials such as heavy flags or brick. The price of using concrete imprinted pavers and installation is usually somewhere in the middle. If you've decided to hire a contractor to do the work, examine some of his completed projects. When you've located a workman whose finished projects please you, have him write out an estimate that includes all parts and labor. Then, be prepared to wait several months for the job to begin. Those who are talented are usually in high demand.

4. Garden Rooms:

Thinking of your garden in terms of separate outdoor rooms is an interesting concept, quite fashionable in current landscape circles. Enthusiasts suggest that it is desirable to separate each and every garden area by means of hedges, walls, or fences-- but it can be overdone. If your fences have seen better days, your walls are in a state of collapse, or you are simply tired of pruning formal hedges once, twice, even three times each growing season, the time has come to consider alternate methods of arranging your garden. Of course, if you are determined to maintain a formal development, then by all means repair the divisions returning them to a decent condition. Remember, though, that formal means symmetrical, and that usually demands a high degree of maintenance. It is the naturalistic garden that often benefits the most from decreasing its number of "rooms."

How well I remember a long, narrow city garden in South Africa that was divided into many tight, complex compartments—the antithesis of naturalism. I get a feeling of claustrophobia when merely recalling all those cubbyholes and the fussy care that each required to keep it neat. What we should all seek in a garden is a feeling of spaciousness. If your present garden is one series of cubbyholes after another, it may be time to remove barriers that serve little purpose. Why not confine full enclosure only to those areas where it is necessary?

For example, some time in the future, you might want to build a swimming pool with its own cabana. Most likely, because of a town or city ordinance, the pool will require complete fencing. Already, you will have a necessary enclosure. Then, too, there are utilitarian areas that you will want to hide behind a fence or wall unless their appearance doesn't bother you. Removing unnecessary barriers is the kind of spatial improvement employed by the house architect who enhances convenience and beauty by removing a wall between two small rooms to create one large, expansive multipurpose room.

You should ask yourself: must you, should you, will you enclose every distinct part of your garden? Few things in life are cut-and dried, and this is especially true when considering opening up all the enclosed parts of your garden.

On the other hand think a bit about a concept that the Japanese call " miegakure," meaning "hide and seek." When all of a garden can be seen at one glance, it loses its air of mystery and enchantment. Hide some, they suggest, so that the viewer will be tempted to slowly seek out the less obvious places of interest. You can do this through the use of long, flowing lines and pathways or lawns that are turned by a few intersecting shrubs, few of them tall and massive, but just high enough to create some concealment. Such an arrangement will allow you to retain that feeling of "I wonder what is around the corner." For this purpose, you might also replace tall, pruned hedges with either a small section of fence or moderate-sized shrubs that need little or no pruning.

Some of the most elegant garden features in the world are stone walls, high, four sided enclosures. Yet, they can be a bit much for all except the most enormous spaces. In Europe, very old walls of brick or stone have long been used to surround garden areas. My own preference is for one or two, rather than a four-sided wall. If you should be fortunate enough to have inherited such a structure, let it serve as a magnificent setting for perennial plants allowing the stone or brick to peek through at intervals.

A few years ago, I visited a landscape architect's country property in upper New York State. An old barn once stood several hundred feet from his house. Although the wooden structure was now long gone, part of a tall, picturesque, somewhat crumbling two-sided stone foundation remained. Since it did not seem to be endangering anyone or anything, the architect left it alone and planted an extensive perennial garden in front of it separating the wild from the cultivated. Were it a complete enclosure, this attractive development would not have been seen from the house. Now, it is partially visible in the distance where it bids the visitor to walk a distance to that garden and fully inspect the plantings. What a wonderful focal point! Your garden probably does not have such a wall, but in a large space, you will surely need some sort of dramatic feature that will encourage visitors to explore the far-off corners of your property.

One frequently sees stone piles or walls in New England where farmers, clearing the land, used them as boundary markers. If there is some place on your property that has a pile of gathered rocks, consider it a bonus to be cherished. With the materials already at hand, use them to build a real wall. Just think. If you had planned one from scratch, imagine the labor and expense that would be required just to haul in those materials! With a little practice and much care, constructing dry-laid walls 3' or lower is usually well within the ability of many do-it-yourselfers.

Existing masonry walls sometimes need a bit of repair. An English author suggests that to patch a slightly crumbling mortared wall, you might want to use a lime and sand based filler (rather than cement) to restore its natural beauty. Take care to remove the roots of trees and shrubs that might have crept under and around the wall because they could endanger its stability.

Under most conditions, vegetable gardens need to be tightly enclosed with a fence to keep out marauding animals, and sometimes, they are isolated at a distance from the house. If you are looking to eliminate a few enclosures, one solution (for those who no longer need a large vegetable garden) is to add a few edible plants to your closer ornamental gardens. Lettuce, for example, can be planted early in an area where you usually set out a few annual plants. Rhubarb is a most attractive plant for a perennial border, and oh, so useful as well—if you like the flavor of its cooked red stems! And for the front of a border where a temporary frill is desired, try the plain, ordinary carrot. Its green, lacy leaves are as pretty as any annual. Also a few herbs might be used on the border's edge. For years, I grew ornamental chives *(Allium schoenoprasum)* for their pretty, long blooming rosy-purple flowers as well as edible foliage.

Growing a few vegetables in containers, possibly placing them on your patio, is another way of having your vegetables without fencing that distant plot. There are quite a few to-mato varieties that can be set in very large containers placed close to your house. This will surely make it easier for you to keep an eye on both watering and animal pests. As you grow older, this will be appreciated all the more, and save you the frequent trudging back and forth to a distant vegetable patch.

5. Unlovely Utilities:

As you work on your site plan, you may be surprised at how many areas really need to be enclosed. Already your expansive look may be in jeopardy. The trick is to use enclosure only when it serves a distinct purpose. Aim for the minimum so that your garden will look as spacious as possible.

Calling the garden "a yard" is like referring to your pet as "that animal." Both terms are too prosaic to describe those things we love so well. Yet, there are unlovely but functional utility areas on every property that can be thought of as yards within a garden. Placing them on a plan will help you to separate the necessary from the ornamental.

Here are some of those you might have: electric generator, air conditioner unit, pool filter, trash cans, dog run, children's play, transplanting bench, cold frame, compost heap, and tool shed. Some will not concern you; others should be fenced in purely for conceal-ment. Some, such as a cold frame or storage shed, are telling features of your work that you might not want to hide. Happily, many enclosures can perform double-duty as an attrac-tive feature.

Many of these utility necessities add nothing to the aesthetics of a place. A generator and a pool filter must have complete protection from the elements and will need some sort of constructed enclosure. An air conditioner does not need such protection, but if you have one on an outside house wall, do not make the mistake of trying to conceal it with living plants. Its dispersal of warm, moist air will, in time, kill off all close plantings. A low concealment fence may be all that you need as the units are usually no taller than 3'.

There is nothing attractive about trash receptacles. In some areas, underground storage pits are allowed which adequately keep the cans out of sight. Wherever they are located, let it be a place that is convenient for both you and the service company that empties them, and this sometimes requires a compromise.

On properties small or large, where you have a utilitarian-looking fence serving as an outdoor dog run, you might want to consider, instead, underground wired perimeter fencing. It will keep your pet safely within your boundary lines. Cats are a different story. When they are allowed to roam outdoors, as is often the case where there is infrequent road traffic, no type of fencing will keep them within property boundaries. Outdoors, cats cannot be contained, although the older they are, the closer to home they seem to stay. How well they defeat fencing was demonstrated to us one day when my husband and I were picking fruit within our tightly netted "blueberry house." There she was, our cat, inside with us. How she gained entry was a mystery.

Children's play is quite another matter, and when they are old enough to be left alone for a while unsupervised, it is still a good idea to be able to see them through the windows of your home with an unrestricted view rather than confining them to a fenced-in area. Youngsters will be all the more content to play in your garden if it has an adequate lawn. If every section of your property is in asphalt, concrete, or gravel, realize that these are hard landings for little bottoms, playgrounds not withstanding. (It will also deprive adults from enjoying an occasional sprawl close to nature.) A garden without a lawn might be a plant paradise but it is not the most comfortable place for children's play.

For the smallest fry, jungle gyms on a lawn provide entertainment for hours, but children grow up all too quickly and abandon them. The sight of play equipment left unused to rust away can only be described as bleak. As you construct your plan on paper, decide how best to convert this space in the future.

True gardeners will not want to hide a cold frame and/or transplanting bench, but few think that a compost heap looks beautiful. Yet, to the horticulturally minded, this source of organic material is as necessary to gardening as milk, eggs, and sugar is to a baker. If placed at a great distance, the pile will become more and more inconvenient as we grow older. Move it closer, but fence it in, possibly with a gate at the entrance.

When a fence is necessary to hide the utilitarian, consider it a backdrop for displaying a fine plant specimen. If you wish, you might want to espalier one magnificent plant against it. (To espalier is to train a tree or shrub on a flat plane in a predetermined pattern). Or, in a space with plenty of sunshine, face the fence with an elegant flowering vine. Any one of the hybrid clematis will probably do if some support is provided. In a shady place, you might prefer the climbing hydrangea, *(H. anomala petiolaris)* a self-clinger but a slow starter.

A gorgeous concealing vine that I once grew, the early spring flowering *Clematis montana rubens*, covered the so-so trellising on the side of our back steps. I planted it in conjunction with a later blooming hybrid. As attractive as the vine was with profuse pale pink blossoms, it became too heavy for its support. Then, too, since both types of clematis required pruning at different seasons, I had great difficulty telling them apart when dormant; the hybrid requires pruning in mid-March. Eventually, I removed montana leaving behind the midsummer bloomer. Lesson learned—plant only a single type of clematis in a somewhat restricted space! In time, one healthy clematis, regardless of its stated mature height in reference books, might fill in a good-sized area.

Where there is already an existing wooden fence that sags in places, do not assume that the fence, itself, has to go. Examine it carefully. It may be that the timber uprights are rotting and new weather-resistant posts will do the job of raising the fence upright. Stain or paint might also renew longevity and good looks.

If your garage has become a catchall for an ever-increasing variety of tools, you might want to get better organized by acquiring a new detached storage shed. Today, there are many interesting prefabricated structures, which, incidentally, might also serve to block an unwanted view. Painted to coordinate with your home, there's no need to hide such a structure because the right shed can be quite decorative. One gardener that I know uses the façade of his shed for a collection of old garden implements. Another development that I once visited had a large mirror on one outside shed wall to expand the image of the flower display in front of it. One's imagination is the prime factor when planning an addition. Many utilitarian features can be both practical and ornamental.

If this is your new-old house, it is very important that you check with the previous owners to discover where there are underground water, sewer/septic tank, gas/oil, and electrical lines so that when digging in new territory, you do not damage them. Repairing them is a maintenance project that you could well do without.

6. Windbreaks and Shade:

Think next about plant utility as opposed to constructed utility. We sometimes consider all plants to be strictly ornamental, but this is not always the case; some may serve as a windbreak. For example: Cut down a hedge of ugly, overgrown conifers, and after every storm, this newly exposed part of your property might become torn and tattered. Then, too, plants in the path of this windbreak, even those that you thought were perfectly hardy, might also begin to suffer as colder air than ever before sweeps down upon them in the winter. If you anticipate this as a problem, relocate another windbreak of handsome conifers on your plan in a similar but slightly distant location from the original planting. Then wait a few years for the new windbreak to mature before tearing down the old.

The same kind of thinking can be applied to a shade tree. If you remove a large, unattractive tree that is close to your patio, the area may become so hot and sunny that you are no longer able to dine alfresco at certain times of the day. This being the case, draw on your plan the location of a new tree to take its place. Where to place it? Decide the hours of the day when you are most likely to use the patio, and if you're particularly observant about the movement of the sun, site the new tree to shade the area at that time of the day. Meanwhile, gradually prune away the branches of the old removing it completely only when the substitute tree has grown enough to provide some shade. Sun umbrellas are fun and pretty, but for shade, there's nothing quite like Mother Nature's most sublime production—the tree!

7. Privacy:

Privacy is something that we all crave in our gardens. Tall, tightly pruned conifers spaced close together to form a hedge have long been considered the ultimate privacy shield. Gardeners throughout the world are forever clipping and shearing these hedges into a screen that looks as though it had been pressed by a steam roller. In most parts of our country, many fine-needled conifers come through repeated shearings in good shape, but I will have none of this. Instead, I prefer a less manicured, more naturalistic solution. Spacing a variety of conifers 7-8' apart at least, will eventually result in a long lasting privacy shield without much pruning, but it will take some time to achieve such cover

If you have a pruned hedge, whether deciduous or coniferous, and it has long been maintained in top-notch condition, and it is, indeed, giving you needed privacy, then you will probably want to continue the high maintenance it requires. Hedges look best, I think, in formal gardens where maintenance has become routine. Professional gardeners love them because it insures their employment at least once, twice, or even three times a growing season. If the hedges are tall, pruning them is a formidable task for the do-it-yourself homeowner. Climbing up on a ladder, shears in hand, is one of the most dangerous practices in gardening. If you, as well as your garden, are in your senior years, you will probably want to concentrate on other, safer, gardening tasks.

Should you decide to take down such a tall hedge, first try leaving a few single plants here and there that look reasonably well when freed from their surrounding neighbors. Then, instead of shearing them, let the remaining plants grow back into informal shapes, hoping that those at the beginning and the end of the row, at least, will fill in. While this treatment may not work well, you have little to lose by trying it. Alternately, after removing the hedge completely, plant and space well apart replacement ornamentals that mature at a height that is acceptable to you.

Many deciduous shrubs have a great deal to offer as a screen, especially when they are most needed during the growing season. You can be highly selective deciding which species requires minimum pruning and yet, have exactly the growing habit that you would like…arching, or horizontally spreading, or pyramidal, or columnar, etc. Small trees, also, especially those that branch low to the ground, may be used effectively for screening. If space allows, and you want more of a barrier, a second, lower tier of shrubs can be placed in front of the backdrop planting. As a whole, most deciduous shrubs need only a season or two to fill in sufficiently as a privacy hedge. Conifers are usually slower for use as a screen..

Where space is limited, or where all-year privacy is desired quickly, some sort of fencing will probably be necessary. By and large, Americans are not nearly as addicted to complete property fencing as British gardeners. Perhaps we feel more comfortable singing "don't fence me in!" Unfortunately, incursions by pestiferous animals, particularly white-tailed deer, are making some sort of fencing almost mandatory in many parts of our country, so perhaps we are changing our tune.

The cultivated areas of our own property, Frog Pond Farm, are now surrounded with heavy-duty polypropylene see-through fencing in many places, and board fencing in others. Perhaps you do not have deer problems, but rather, a busy road or the sight of a neighbor's house that you wish to screen out. In this case, select the type of fencing that best fits in with the style of your house, and use it in sections rather than all over the property.

Don't overlook the possibility that there might be a distant view outside your property that is well worth framing, and maybe, now is the time to clear away some of your own plants that are hiding it. Perhaps what you want most is a property separation boundary. Many moderately tall deciduous shrubs might fit the bill. The old fashioned Spiraea *x vanhouttei* is still a good bet for this purpose. Some shrub roses can also be satisfactory as a hedge and are worth investigating. When researching the faults and attributes of these roses, try to select those that are repeat bloomers, relatively free of insects and diseases, and only moderately rapid growers. Where hardiness is a problem, look to purchase roses that are propagated on their own root rather than from grafts. There is less of a chance of losing them in a very severe winter.

Before proceeding with any of these suggested approaches, draw the new look on your site plan. It will help you to envision the consequences of removing old plants too quickly or allowing certain species to remain that must be pruned constantly to keep them at a reasonable height.

8. Garden Paths:

A woman I know lives on an estate, loves and works in her garden, but is unable to do much walking. She uses a golf cart to take her from here to there. Stairs and steps have been replaced by ramps. Paved walks are everywhere. All of us, whether we are handicapped or not, need to easily navigate walks leading to the doors of our homes. On difficult sites where drainage is poor, pressure treated deck-like boards raised 6" or so off the ground may do the trick. This describes our rear walk at Frog Pond Farm which was once part of a brook, and where the soil is still wet. My husband used 1x6 pressure treated lumber which he cut into 5' long boards, some wedge shaped to round a corner.

Auxiliary paths are something else. It all depends on your garden, and they surely are the stuff of popular attention at present. Yet, many paths are not always essential, especially in the country. Most of our present pathways (except to the rear and front of our house) are lawns. These lawns, as imperfect as they may be, smell fragrant, are soft underfoot, beautiful in color, and, in essence, a natural way of moving around our garden. Their only drawback is that in the depths of winter, the grass can get water logged, then freezes into a dangerously slippery state.

Our own location, in a cold little valley, means that the greater part of our garden cannot be trod upon until meltdown and spring returns. Constructed paths everywhere would also freeze and be of little use during winter. When our lawns and patio are not snow covered, they are slick with ice. If your climate allows it, and you are able and willing to work in the garden in cold weather, then adding auxiliary paths here and there makes good sense.

For use during grass mowing season, I sank stepping stones at one turn in the lawn. The mower can move nicely right over them. In another place, I allowed moss to grow into a transition area, the most suitable bit of path that I could select for entrance to our wild-flower area. Before winter sets in, though, the area must be carefully raked of leaves. And then, there is one place where I needed a very short bit of path within a groundcover area so that I wouldn't flatten the plants when stepping on them. Again, a few stepping stones took care of the matter very well indeed.

In more formal gardens, or any place where it is difficult to maneuver, or in places where not enough space has been allowed to use a wheelbarrow or tractor and cart, a wider auxiliary path might be needed. A few possibilities are: brick set in sand, asphalt, pea gravel, crushed rock, or wood rounds set in gravel. For temporary pathways or in a naturalistic garden, mulch-like materials might serve as well, such things as small nuggets of pine bark, wood chips, pine needles, buckwheat hulls, licorice bark, cocoa or peanut shells. The materials probably depend on what is easily and inexpensively available in your area, are of a consistency that will permit a smooth passage for wheels, and blend in unobtrusively with your plantings. Straight lines and mortared brick through a wildflower patch, for example, contradict the natural feeling that a gardener may be trying to convey.

The edging that holds a path in place is also important. Small, rough-cut level field-stones arranged in a random pattern do an admirable job of separating border and lawn.

However, if your path is adjacent to lawns on both sides, nothing further may be necessary.

At our first home, I needed to reach my greenhouse in all weather. It was 100' in back of our house. A tight budget allowed for only a path composed of a 2 to 3" layer of woodchips over newspapers. This path bordered a long perennial bed. As the chips disintegrated, I dug up parts of the path and added this organic matter to the perennial planting, a compost heap in situ, one might say. Although the path needed to be resurfaced with more chips after every few years, this was not as laborious as carting endless wheelbarrows of compost to enrich the perennial bed soil. Meanwhile, the well drained path was pleasant to walk on, dry in winter, and really quite satisfactory. If those who gardened here after me wished to do so, they could easily enlarge the perennial area into the path and create a new, more permanent walkway in front of it.

There is one area at Frog Pond Farm that I like to check after the turn of the year, but am able to do so only if there is a January thaw. It is then that I try to get a look at our rock garden. Because of this, I have a narrow path of ¾" gravel surrounding this raised rock bed. Gravel, in imitation of the natural scree on a mountainside, surely belongs near a rock development. Sloping sites, however, present a special problem because with every rain, gravel washes away unless boxed tightly in place.

If your garden has existing paths that you intend to replace after renovating an area, don't be in a hurry to tear them out. As dilapidated as they are, they might still be more serviceable than their muddy base while you are moving heavy plants or other materials elsewhere in your garden. Save removal and reconstruction of new paths as a concluding project.

If lawns are not sufficient for you as walkways, and you decide to construct entirely new paths, traverse the track around your property many times before determining where they are most needed. Having arrived at a logical traffic pattern, install them gradually. If you are still not certain where to locate them, you could create paths made with temporary materials before you settle on permanent paths and materials.

In renovating an older garden where patio paving, garden structures, windbreaks, hedges, fences, utility enclosures, privacy shields, and paths have either disappeared or need some work, keep in the back of your mind your prime goal: lower maintenance raises garden pleasure. By making needed changes and repairs once and for all, the time you save will be better spent in the garden relaxing with friends and family.

CHAPTER IX
PERPLEXING PERENNIALS

Natalia Petrioagla

CHAPTER IX
Perplexing Perennials

How well I remember that one glorious clump of peonies growing in the backyard of our small city home. I marveled when every May, it sported uncountable dozens of fragrant, double pink blooms without ever being watered, fertilized, or even noticed by anyone but me, perhaps a child of ten years. The plant was a true, long-lasting herbaceous perennial.

Yet, the lifecycle of many perennials can be perplexing. Some verbascums, foxgloves, and campanulas, for example, return in full glory every year while others of the same species are biennials—that is, they grow the first year, then bloom, seed, and die the second. Then there are those herbaceous perennials, such as hybrid delphiniums, that can be glorious their first year in my country garden, but very few plants, if any, return for a repeat performance. Our soils and climate cut short their lives.

According to the dictionary, an herbaceous perennial should endure for at least three seasons. Yet, in spite of our best cultural efforts, not all of these plants are even that obliging. A gardener looking for long-term reliability needs to access the longevity of all his existing plants as well as his planned acquisitions.

One of the most pleasing things about the older garden is that it may already contain some steadfast perennials, the kind that we can depend on like old, comforting friends. Whether you have only a few healthy clumps or a large collection of perennials, let these hardy specimens be the starting point for your redesign, the anchor on which to base your future work. A first task, in gardens set for renovation, is reorganization.

In nature, herbaceous perennials grow in a variety of places, such as the floor of a woodland, or on the sunny side of a clearing, or in a prairie-like glade, or in swampy places, or open meadows, or within rocky outcroppings. If any semblance of this kind of terrain already exists in your garden, then that should help you to determine your theme and how best to enhance that theme with perennials that thrive under similar conditions. But for our purposes, let us consider more traditional "beds" or "borders."

All too often, beds are carved within lawns with no relationship to the overall scheme. One sees these cut-outs as circles, squares, kidney shapes, whatever the gardener can devise. Originally conceived by earlier gardeners as a means of displaying annual and tropical flowers, beds are also used today for groupings of perennials accompanied by spring flowering bulbs. Sometimes, these shapes are given the definition "island beds." Many perennials may be perfectly lovely in a climate more temperate than mine, but where winters are long and frigid, their dormant stage contributes nothing of beauty to our landscaping. Although some are evergreen, most are not, and must be protected with a mulch or conifer boughs to guard against upheaval from freezing and thawing. This can look forlorn, indeed, for five or six months of the year.

If you use perennials in beds, how much better it is to connect them to a side border so that the whole appearance is a swooping, swirling mass rather than an isolated island. And/or, if possible, add a small tree or two, even a few low shrubs, to give year-round substance to the bed rather than the view of a solidly mulched area within a lawn.

Perennial borders are usually sideliners. Their prime purpose is to display flowers in an artistically pleasing manner. The border, itself, is the long slice of earth that fronts a wall, a fence, tall shrubbery, or a hedgerow. It can be planted entirely with herbaceous perennials or, as is more common in a naturalistic garden, combined with conifers, trees, or shrubs that all compliment one another. A fine border can be one of horticulture's greatest achievements, something many gardeners strive to create, but careful soil preparation and plant selection are necessary for a good result as well as a willingness on the gardener's part to keep the border free of weeds, enrich the soil frequently, and divide most of the plants every few year. A tall order!

Let us suppose that you've taken a close look at the scattered perennial clumps here and there in your garden, and you've decided that when in bloom, there are far too few plants to sustain more than a casual interest. This may be the time to consolidate clumps from several areas into one border, especially if you have an ideal sunny location in mind...the sunnier the better. It is at this point that your imagination takes over. You will have tall flowers, short flowers, and those in between; flowers of brilliant colors or flowers that are more subtle pastels; flower colors that appear and are coordinated to bloom with those of backdrop shrubs; spike flowers or daisy flowers or combinations of many shapes. In fact, you want so many flowers that you could fill every vase in your house and still have a bountiful outdoor display.

Perhaps you have a distant boundary line fence. If you will use the fence as a backdrop, you already have the start of a fine perennial border. Now you look at those few clusters of daylilies near your lamppost. You remember that near your back door is a nice patch of blue salvia. You could move both of them into that perennial border and you will, indeed, have the beginnings of something special. Should you then hurry to lay out the border's length and width?

Before your creative ambitions run away with you, be sure you understand the future "care" factor. All too many of us get carried away by wanting to replicate the exuberant double perennial borders we have seen in botanical gardens or in estate gardens tended by full time horticultural professionals. The do-it-yourself hobby gardener should realize that no matter how many moments we can devote to gardening, it is our avocation, not our vocation. When our cravings exceed the time and energy we are able to give to a project, we often attempt to do more than we can manage, and the results can be disappointing. Rather than throwing in the trowel, redesign the layout of your border, whether it is new or old, so that you can manage it easily. (See Chapter X)

If there is already an existing border on your property but it looks tired and humdrum, determine which are the pivotal perennials that have made this garden a success in the past. These are the ones to repeat, perhaps with some of the newer, more unusual cultivars, and plant them in quantity, over and over again.

Every long-time gardener knows that from early winter through the spring, he or she will be deluged with a great number of mail order plant catalogues, especially those for perennials. Within our fingertips are possibilities for purchasing flowering plants that might make our gardens better. Regardless of how filled our beds or borders might be, is there one among us who will let a season pass without adding something new?

Throughout winter in the greater part of the United States, the ardent gardener clings to these "possibilities" like a drowning person to his life raft. Plotting to plant new additions becomes irresistible, inescapable. Early every spring, I mail out at least one small perennial plant order even if my greenhouse (or cold frame) is already bulging with young plants that I have propagated from seed or cuttings. The longer cold weather lingers into March, then April, the longer becomes my order because, to me, there are probably many exquisite newly introduced gems that I really must have to add excitement to my borders. If you are thinking of renovating your borders, and even your pivotal plants no longer please you, then your list will probably exceed the budget that you have set.

Yet, experience tells us that each new specimen will demand more attention its first year than those that are fully established. Overly ambitious new plantings can lead to many losses, so be prepared to spend more time that season working in the border then elsewhere on your property. Many perennials do not look their best when first set in place, and quite a few will not even bloom their first year in your garden. Keep this in mind if you're thinking of tossing out all the old at one time and starting anew.

Like other gardeners, spectacular photographs attract my attention, but what I see on those catalogue pages are mostly close-ups of blossoms. And who can resist those pretty faces? Annual and perennial flowers are often photographed with a macro lens to magnify their beauty, but even the most humble plant looks enchanting when the camera moves in a foot or so from the flowers. My husband and I know that it is easy to capture beauty in a close-up, but far more difficult to photograph the complete plant from its anchor in the earth to its tallest stems. The overall character of a perennial is best seen if you are standing at a slight distance from each fully grown specimen. Minute details, as observed in close-ups, are more useful to trained horticulturists or to botanists who count such things as stamens and pistils, so select your new plants with their overall appearance in mind.

Catalogue photographs are usually accompanied by a description and sometimes, a little cultural information. Still, this can leave one with a distorted image. That was my experience the first time that I planted the cinquefoil *Potentilla atrosanguineum* 'Monarch's Velvet'. The strawberry-like foliage is quite attractive, but the long, wayward stems are far too lax to suit my taste. Then, too, the red blooms, although a good, rich color, look much larger and more significant in a photograph than the real thing. It taught me that when dealing with unfamiliar and expensive new perennials, it is best to first plant one clump in a nursery bed strictly as a trial before adding the new to my borders. That is what I call hedging your bets!

When renovating flower gardens, experienced gardeners think twice about climatic requirements and hardiness of unfamiliar plants. Yet, prevailing conditions can and do change with time! Fifteen years ago, our own garden was regularly subjected -15 to −17 degree temperatures every winter. For many years now, the thermometer has not plunged lower than zero. What will next year bring? We should be aware of the fact that planting a Zone 6 perennial in what was once Zone 5, may be a gamble, Fortunately, if a perennial proves to be somewhat tender for you, it might survive for a number of years when the winters are unusually mild.

If your renovated perennial areas are growing in size rather than receding, and they truly please you, face up to the realization that eventually, many will need division. Senior gardeners often wonder how on earth they'll find the strength to dig up those hefty clumps, divide them, and reset the divisions before they wilt. If this describes your situation, then this may be the time in your life to call upon part time help. Consider the search for help even more important than locating an elusive plant. In some areas, part-time labor is readily available, but in others, finding a competent assistant may not be so easy. It is usually no problem at all hiring someone to mow our lawns, but where are we to find a once-a-week gardener who is knowledgeable enough to help us divide, weed, water, spray, fertilize, and deadhead our perennials as the need arises? Good gardeners can be as scarce as a sunny day in January. Part of the solution may be for you to provide hands-on training to a willing applicant, and after he or she has grown proficient, you can hope that their tenure with you will be long-lasting.

Perhaps the most perplexing thing about perennials is that even in one garden, the performance of the same species can vary from place to place. Where the soil is heavy, a perennial can grow unexpectedly tall and lanky and need staking. In a sandy, gritty area, the same plant may grow shorter and more compact. Gardeners must admit that all too often, their efforts are a matter of trial and error.

Another thing that all perennial gardeners soon learn is that like the members of a family, not all the species in the same genus enjoy the same conditions. The true geranium, for example, not the potted pelargonium also called Geranium, comes to mind as one of our most useful perennials. Yet, I have found that the so-called "big root" geranium of Southern Europe *(G. macrorrhizum)* thrives only where there is light shade and moisture during the summer. On the other hand, the bloody cranesbill *(G. sanguinium lancastriensis)* needs a well- drained, sunny place such as a rock garden.

The most interesting thing about many perennials is that within one genus, we can often find the exact species and/or cultivar that will suit our purpose. *Geranium* x 'Dilys', for example, has long, trailing stems and a sprawling habit. I'm not sure that I like its wandering stems in my border, but it would probably look great dangling from a retaining wall. On the other hand, *G. oxonianum* 'Wargrave Pink' grows as a vigorous mound ideal for the front of a border as does *G. cantabrigiense* 'Biokova' and many other true geraniums. Before selecting those that seem likely candidates, it pays to spend a little extra time studying that perennial's habits. Use a reference book that gives you this information.

Even more perplexing is the phrase "grows well near water." It all depends on the situation. I once planted Eastern marsh marigolds, *Caltha palustris*, in the small bed adjacent to our rear garden pool. Oddly, the situation was far too dry for them. Before they faded away, I transplanted them to the center of our brook where they grow nicely each year. They are held in place from the rushing waters by a low wall of rocks, but the catalogue description might better have read, "needs sopping wet conditions."

Maximizing the conditions of the "dry" poolside bed, I added some sand and gravel and was then able to plant several pretty rock garden type plants such as the pink thrift, *Armeria juniperifolia*. It's always a bonus when you are able to convert an unlikely space to suit a species that you want to grow.

And then, there's our narrow west-facing "white flowered" bed below our dry-laid rock walls. It tends to be soggy during late winter and early spring. Yet, year after year, it supports three dwarf white flowering roses. *Rosa* 'Alba Meidiland.' Most roses, of course, need well-drained soil, so their survival here is a mystery to me. Many companion plants that I've tried here below the wall were short lived until I finally discovered that *Sidalcea candida, Filipendula ulmaria*, and white flowering astilbes reappear every spring. My answer is that sometimes, you can expect the unexpected and when successful, plant more of the same.

Following zonal maps as though they were road maps does not always work well either. They are but a rough guide. These U.S. Department of Agriculture's climatic maps are based on the range of average minimal temperatures for fifteen geographical zones in the U.S. and Canada. There is also a separate Plant Heat Zone map for twelve geographical areas based on the average number of days per year when summer temperatures run as high or higher than 86 degrees. These maps are, indeed, helpful although neither was meant to be a perfect guide to plant hardiness because so many other factors are involved.

For example, while the average January temperature in Colorado is similar to that in Northern New Jersey, Colorado's drier climate produces only 16.6" of rainfall per year while our part of New Jersey can usually count on about 50" of annual precipitation. This alone makes a great difference in plant survivability. Weeks of summer humidity in the Northeast, rarely experienced in Colorado, can ruin many a coveted perennial here, or at the very least, leave it in a bedraggled state, while Coloradans can grow a whole host of magnificent mountain plants. Yet, there are many perennials that surprise me by doing far better in northern New Jersey than references indicate. The lovely *Saxifraga x urbium*, commonly called 'London Pride,' is usually listed as hardy to only Zone 7, but it does splendidly in a lightly shaded spot in my garden. The same can be said of the strawberry geranium, *Saxifraga sarmentosa*. Then, too, many of my northern New Jersey friends complain that in their soils, they cannot grow the southeastern native Stokes aster, *Stokesia laevis*. For me, it is almost a take-over plant. Perennial gardening is full of perplexing situations.

My own two curved perennial borders face each other with a meadow lawn 20' wide between them. The borders are composed of backdrop shrubs, perennials for three seasons, plus adjacent raised rock beds. Upon our arrival at the scene thirty-four years ago, I began this area as a half acre shrub and tree nursery for my landscape business. After twenty years, the stock was dispersed, and I then drew a scaled design plan on paper for an ornamental garden. For awhile, I had to work around the few shrubs that remained, but eventually, most were transplanted elsewhere and I started afresh. This was the time for soil fertility renewal.

The bucket of our big old farm tractor was used to rework the skimpy layer of topsoil into the new borders. As I discovered, many trees and shrubs (including hardy azaleas and rhododendrons) are not really as demanding of the deep, enriched soil conditions needed for choice perennials. Double digging by hand, so often recommended, was not an option here because below a foot or so, we hit solid bedrock. Above it, our soils are heavy, rocky clay.

Nevertheless, applications of copious amounts of well rotted horse manure and compost resulted in a reasonably good initial display. We incorporated these materials into the existing soil with a rototiller and then raked away large stones. If the area were smaller, we probably would have used a spade and a potato hook, the latter, one of my favorite tools. Remember, when using a tiller, that rocks can damage the blades, so use extreme caution. A tiller cannot dig deeper than 8", so you may also have to do some hand digging. After we accomplished this, we dug large planting holes even for small perennials, and then set each into the slightly amended soil. Since I had started many of the plants from seed or cuttings the year before, I gave every perennial plenty of space. As expected, the first year of their growth produced rather spotty results. I spent that summer on my hands and knees constantly weeding. The following year was not too bad; the weeds were fewer, the perennials filled in nicely, and I was almost ready to call myself Gertrude Jekyll. But by the third and fourth year, I relinquished that title. Some plants needed staking (a chore that I despise), some looked scraggly due to deer nibbling and a long drought, and some were so aggressive that they were crowding out their nicer neighbors. Others became so mildewed that they had to be sprayed constantly with a fungicide. It seemed as though the misfortunes of Job were upon me and I was ready to pull the whole thing out and let the meadow grass take over.

Eventually, after deer inhibiting fences were installed, I removed the inferior and sought out other plants that did better in our heavy clay soils. In most places, constant thinning, division, and soil amendments are still necessary to keep the borders looking reasonably good. A few borderline plants such as *Artemisia* 'Powis Castle' with lovely silver foliage, die out here when the winter is unusually severe. To preserve them, I once bothered to reroot and grow them afresh every year. Others, such as many of the finer delphiniums, need skillful staking. I decided that for me, at this time in my life, these species were not worth the trouble.

Happily, not every plant must be divided every year, so if you are looking into lower maintenance, the following are the ones that should occupy your largest areas: peonies can live indefinitely without division; iris, especially the two delightful species *Iris ensata* and *I. sibirica*, require it only after four or five four years. Daylilies (*Hemerocallis*) get larger and more floriferous every year and should be divided only if they outgrow their space. Moderately tall sedums and purple coneflowers (*Echinacea*) can go a very long time without divisions. These perennials might be called the ironclads of our perennial genera, the basic components of sunny borders almost everywhere even where soil conditions are less than ideal. There are, of course, many others that are equally as carefree. Finding those are suitable under your conditions is like solving a crossword puzzle.

All herbaceous borders will probably need some soil amending each year, unless, of course, you live in the Garden of Eden. That, to me, means sandy loam, well drained, rockless soils (gravelly for alpines) in an area where the temperature never sinks lower than 10 degrees F. nor rises above 80 degrees F. I have never gardened in a place with these conditions. Maybe you are luckier.

If the beds or borders you're renovating are choked with perennial weeds such as thistle, an herbicide like Roundup will probably do a good job of eradicating them. If you prefer not to use chemicals, then here is another method that I have tried: First, cut all stems to the ground and add well rotted compost or manure to the area, as much as your supply permits. Mushroom soil is also very good, if you can find it. Next, place thick sheets of newspaper over this area. Then cover with cutouts of 4 mil black polyethylene. Under this, deprived of light, the weeds will slowly die. Sometimes, the process may take as long as a year to rid the area of the toughest roots, and only then can the poly be removed safely. While it takes patience to wait it out before replanting, an eventual weed-free area might be worth it.

Two other factors come into play when you are renovating an existing perennial area: our changing tastes and increasing shade. Once, I grew *Rudbeckia fulgida* 'Goldstrum,' the vigorous black-eyed Susan, in a large mass along our driveway. The display was colorful, long in bloom, and definitely low on maintenance. However, after many years, I tired of their brash golden color. Not only that but I noticed how plant vigor was gradually diminishing. This was because the nearby flowering dogwood had grown much larger and was giving the Susans too much shade. Out came these perennials and the soil was then enriched with a great deal of peat moss and compost. When the tilth was thick and fluffy, in went a bed of pink and rose astilbes. A shallow mulch of chopped leaves helps to retain soil moisture during the summer. During the common midsummer dry period, the astilbes must be thoroughly watered, but their beautiful foliage and lovely flowers are well worth the trouble. Besides, in some years, Mother Nature will take care of the watering with frequent showers on many summer days and nights.

If you want or need to make some big changes when renovating your perennial areas, don't just rush out to purchase any or all the plants that sound appealing. First, ask your-self these basic questions about the perennials being considered: Will they receive their required amount of sun or shade? Will they stand erect without staking? Will they survive fairly well under brief flooding or drought conditions—the latter, if it does not rain for two weeks? Without corrective spraying, will the plants usually be free of any devastating insect and disease attacks? Will they be perfectly hardy in winter with a light mulch if you cannot count on a constant blanket of snow? Are they of a shape and color that will not be difficult to combine with the best of what you already have? Given adequate fertility, are they vigorous growers, yet without overly aggressive tendencies? For lower maintenance, narrow your choices to plants that have these attributes. When a bed or border reaches a desirable stage, perhaps we should all learn that: The time has come to leave well enough alone.

In the next chapter, I'll go into more specifics about plant selection and management of newly renovated perennial areas.

CHAPTER X
AWAY WITH THE FUSSY, ON WITH THE ENDURING

CHAPTER X
Away With the Fussy, On With the Carefree

Let us say that you've recently moved into a new–old home and now, you tell yourself, you might have been a little too optimistic about caring for its large perennial border. Yet, it would be a shame to dismantle it completely when so many of the plants are growing nicely. What to do? Don't let any "aficionado" tell you that the border must be 10' wide by 100' long. What it must be is a size that you can enjoyably manage, perhaps smaller. Small, when well managed, is often better than large and weedy. Just think—dynamite comes in small packages!

Here are some of your options:

1. Reduce the length of your border to 25, 30, or 40'and its width to no more than 6', not an unreasonable size for a fine display. Plant the now empty backdrop with a few shrubs or conifers of a moderate height; and/or

2. Take out any tall, fussy perennials and replace them with neat flowering shrubs 4 to 5' in height and width. You might want to look into the most compact of hardy species such as abelias, barberries, daphnes, deutzias, spiraeas, and dwarf forms of fothergillas and hydrangeas. These would look splendid when combined with other perennials; and/or

3. Replace part of the border with a strip of lawn along the back. It will not only cut down on cultivated space but also make it easier for you to work without stepping on plants; and/or

4. Instead of low perennials at the front, use flowering groundcover types, such as various forms of thyme, dwarf iris, moss pinks, sedums, and veronicas. Some forms of *Dianthus* can also be used for this purpose, but do be aware that the interiors of both cheddar pinks *(Dianthus gratianopolitanus)* and cottage pinks *(D. plumarius)* can become perfect beds for every pesky grass seed in the area.

In reducing your perennial areas, most probably you'll be confronted with extra plants that are too good for the compost heap, yet too time consuming to keep. Rather than tossing them out, you might give them to a neighbor or pot them up for your organization's plant sale, or tuck a few between some of your other shrubs. True, the later may be a short-term solution as the shrubs grow together, but it will offer an immediate remedy. I've done this with some of my extra daylilies, planting several of the same variety here and there between existing azaleas. The shrubs, themselves, although of good size, continue to grow and try to crowd out the perennials, but a bit of azalea pruning during the summer should keep the daylilies in good shape—for a short time anyway.

If you decide to eliminate the borders entirely, then you might consider planting the space with conifers or broadleaf evergreens which require less care than herbaceous plants.

Or, as several friends of mine have done, plant low flowering perennials to skirt unusual dwarf conifer specimens. Another friend combines boulders and alpine-type perennials. Planting only perennials en masse is merely one way of treating them, the way I personally prefer given the care time and the space. What makes visiting other people's gardens so interesting is that every individual gardener shows his or her imagination clearly in how plants are combined. Superb selection is the key to every work of art, from the composition of a painting to the notes of music in a sonata or a symphony. The biggest difference between these arts is that a garden is never complete. There is no final achievement and its maintenance is never permanent.

If and when you've eliminated some of your fussy perennials that required staking, spraying, or other high maintenance chores, and you've finally accomplished some control over your border, you might try another strategy to add interest to the remaining perennials. Integrate those with attractive dark foliage! Although these plants also flower, it is the color of the leaves that adds all season interest to a garden. In dappled shade, you might try the black snakeroot, *Cimicifuga racemosa* 'Hillside Beauty'. Its dark purple foliage and white flowers are a perfect foil against the green of other plants. Give it rear spacing in a border as the stems can rise to 5 to7'. The 3' loosestrife, *Lysimachia ciliata* 'Atropurpurea', with its bronze foliage and yellow flowers, is a possibility for sunnier places, but watch it because it can become a little too vigorous. The dark purple leafed annual called *Perilla frutescens crispa* seeds around prolifically but is easy to remove remove or transplant. It adds a nice purple-leafed touch to contrast with bright colored perennials. Still another unusual dark touch, if you like ornamental grasses, is the use of *Pennisetum setaceum* 'Atropurpureum' with stems and leaves that are dark purple.

You can also use other hardy ornamental grasses in a variety of situations. Planting groups of one species or cultivar in an area can be highly effective. Be prepared, however, to face what seems to me to be a serious drawback with these grasses; most of them are devilishly difficult to cut down to grade each spring which is part of their cultivation.

In sunny places, there are a great many easy tall sedums that you might try. All have interesting foliage and lovely flowers. The cultivar, *Sedum spectabile* 'Autumn Joy', is effective in leaf and bloom for a very long time near the middle of a border, but if you've seen too much of it in other gardens, you may not be anxious to include it. If this is the case, then look into some of the newer varieties such as *Sedum* 'Meteor', 'Matrona', 'Frosty Morn', 'Brilliant', 'Neon', 'Carmen', or 'Star Dust'. When a perennial is overused, one of its recently introduced cultivars might add just the touch you are looking for.

Sometimes, plants with variegated foliage, if not overdone, can really lighten up a border, especially before or after the other plants are in bloom. *Polemonium* 'Brise d'Anjou' with intricate, yellow edged foliage is one of them although it may not persist after an unusually cold winter. Thus far, I've also tried *Iris ensata* 'Variegata', *Veronica incana* 'Noah Williams', and *Physostegia virginiana* 'Variegata'. The stripes of yellow or white amidst the green are quite lovely, but none of these cultivars, in my experience, are for impatient gardeners. They seem to take quite a few years to mature enough to exhibit their showy presence.

Many a border may suddenly sport self-sown perennial seedlings that can overrun a space if allowed to persist. It is better is to plant them elsewhere as I have done with the perennial foxglove, *Digitalis grandiflora*. I welcome its 2 to 2 ½' stalks with soft, yellow, thimble shaped flowers that appear each year toward the end of June at just the moment when many other perennials are fading. My garden, though, is a naturalistic endeavor where the foxgloves look most appropriate among early wildflowers. They are not for the meek gardener who hates to pull out all the extras, transplanting only some. Nor are they for small gardens with limited perennial areas. The same could be said of columbines *(Aquilegias)* which self-seed and hybridize freely in colors other than you planted. As lovely as they are, columbines can interfere with a planned color scheme in the border, and so are best avoided if you wish to limit your color pallet.

While searching for flowering perennials to plant in sunny places, particularly those with good growing season foliage, look into specific varieties such as alyssum, bergenia, dianthus, some geraniums, iberis, some iris, low phloxes, peonies, and many sedums. These recommendations only scratch the surface. Do be aware that in winter, some of these plants have evergreen foliage, at least in the climate where I live. This is surely a plus compared to the off season barren places left by most perennials.

The older garden, where there are often large trees, frequently becomes too shady for many perennials. This is no cause for despair. Some of the world's most sensational gardens are those created in semi-woodland situations. If the lack of light is not too severe, there are many perennials that actually prefer this condition. Some plants flower early in the season before deciduous trees come into leaf and darken the area below so a little later shade is not a problem. Others sport exquisite foliage that would be quite enough even if the plants never produced dramatic blooms. If encroaching shade mars your existing perennials, then it is time to toss out those languishing sunflowers and in their place, look into these species: asarum, astilbe, bergenia, cyclamen, epimedium, galax, gaultheria, helleborus, hepatica, heucheras, liriope, paxistima, pulmonaria, saxifraga, and tiarella. And then, of course, you can also plant more spring bulbs, ferns, and woodland wildflowers, both native and introduced. Dappled shade is also an excuse to explore that wonderfully varied tribe of perennials called primroses or *Primula*. For a month or more in spring, *P. japonica* lightens up our shady brook at Frog Pond Farm, and other non-fussy species, such as *P. cowichan, P. denticulata, P. sieboldii,* and *P. veris,* are equally at home here.

I have not yet mentioned hostas, those leafy perennials that have, within recent years, become the backbone of many shade gardens. It is no wonder that they are winning so many popularity contests. Of the forty known species, all from the Orient, about a half a dozen species have been so hybridized that that there is scarcely a cultivar without some use somewhere in every temperate garden.

While many hostas prefer slightly damp shade, some will tolerate, even prefer, a little more sun, a handy thing to keep in mind when the area drifts into differing light situations. Unless slugs and/or over-populations of deer are present, they are the perfect solution for areas of your garden where trees and shrubs have grown large and are now shading out perennials that cry out for more sunshine. Hostas can be selected in many sizes. *Hosta* 'Sum and Substance' grows to 3' in height and width, and has a commanding presence. There are also 6-12" little ones, such species as *H longipes, tardiflora,* and *venusta,* that are perfect for edging. Many others of standard size can be located in the marketplace with foliage in every imaginable color combination... shades of green, gray, and blue green, plus a host of variegated forms, but all with the same characteristic paddle-shaped leaves. Give hostas time to develop, though. While they may look a little skimpy the first year or two after planting, they increase in size and beauty with every passing season until their leaves, stretched out in a bed, appear to undulate like the waves of the ocean.

One of the instructions often given as a perennial requirement is "plant in well drained soil." Where this is a problem, and it surely is at Frog Pond Farm, the likely solution is to create raised beds filled with carefully amended soil. Our own low bed, retained with a dry-laid rock wall at the front and old telephone poles at the rear, has permitted me to grow many a perennial that would otherwise languish in ground level borders.

Let us suppose that you have cleaned out an area of unattractive shrubs and trees and now have a whole new bed that you can devote to easy-care, long-in-bloom perennials. It is well to realize that regardless of advertising, no species of perennial (in the greater part of the U.S.) blooms during the entire growing season. Some, though, bloom longer than others. The much-publicized *Coreopsis verticillata* 'Moonbeam' goes on seemingly forever, but only in well drained spaces where there is plenty of sunshine. Before you add more of any particular species or cultivar, it's not a bad idea to tally the length of time your favorite perennials stay in bloom.

Besides the rudbeckias and sedums I mentioned above, the following are among those plants that I have found to be the most carefree and unusually long in bloom in the heavy clay soils of Zones 5 and 6: *Aruncus aesthusifolius, Alchemilla mollis, Anemone vitifolia* 'Robustissima', *Brunnera macrophylla, Chelone lyonii, Chrysanthemum x superbum, Dianthus chinensis* 'Ideal', *Digitalis grandiflora, Echinacea* cultivars, *Geranium endressi* and *sanguineum, Hemerocallis* 'Stella d'oro and H. 'Happy Days', *Helleborus orientalis, Helenium au-*

tumnale, Heliopsis decapetalus, Malva moschata, Veronicastrum virginicum, and *Primulas,* some of which require damp soil *Chelone lyonii,* or pink turtle-head, is a particular favorite of mine. It's closely related to the white flowered native turtle-head growing in waste places here. In my garden, it becomes a huge clump with uncountable flowers that bloom for a long time in late summer.

There are, of course, many other flowering plants that you might try, but the above are those that are almost foolproof in our rather inhospitable clay soils.

If you live in an area where there are still undeveloped places, and reliability and longevity are uppermost in your mind, it's not a bad idea to first see what kind of wildflowers are growing in the vicinity of your home. For example, ox-eye daisies *(Chrysanthemum leucanthemum)* abound in many a sunny field close to Frog Pond Farm. I knew that some of the more refined relatives, such as Shasta daisies *(C. x. superbum),* would probably do well in my garden. And they do. Except for occasional division, the cultivar 'Alaska' has proven to be one of our most carefree, dependable, and vigorous perennials. The small colony that I have established can always be counted on for its lovely midsummer blooming display. As a cut flower, as well, this daisy is long lasting, and for several weeks in a vase, remains as fresh as a you-know-what. Then, too, in wild, shady natural areas, we find bloodroot *(Sanguinaria canadensis).* This native denizen of the verges bordering our tree-lined roads is also quite at home on the north side of our patio.

There are certain tasks that increase flower displays. One of them is deadheading or removing spent flowers soon after they bloom. It's a good idea which sometimes results in repeated bloom later in the season. For me, all too often, deadheading is needed when we're preparing to go on a trip, or out-of-state relatives are visiting and occupy much of my time, or the weather suddenly turns brutally hot and humid. Think of it in this way: Deadheading is not an absolute necessity, and if it is neglected because you're just too busy, don't worry. Just let the plants go to seed. The birds will love you for it.

In alkaline, sandy, or gravely soils, you'll have to follow the advice of others who always work with these conditions. Their list of carefree perennials may be somewhat different than mine. The plants mentioned above are some of those that I have found to be the most carefree in my own Mid-Atlantic garden. That means without the frequent necessity of fertilizing, dividing, pinching, spraying, or staking. As you renovate, let low maintenance plants form the major part of your perennial plantings.

CHAPTER XI
LOVE THAT LAWN

Natalia Petrianyk

CHAPTER XI
Love that Lawn

Imagine, if you will, a warm spring day when the earth is full of delicious fragrances and you have the urge to stretch out on your soft, newly greened grasses. For many homeowners, there is nothing quite like a lawn. Yet, there are those who would, if they could and local ordinances allow for it, substitute gravel for every patch of lawn in their gardens. Gravel has its place, but for the sweet comfort of a close encounter with nature, nothing can compete with your own private lawn.

Some Americans have a love-hate relationship with their lawns. They feel that a garden is not a garden without its patch of green grass, large or small, and that to have one somewhere on their properties is inevitable. On the other hand, they resent spending what seems like an excessive amount of time on lawn maintenance. To them, it seems a far greater chore than any other outdoor task. The true lawn lover, of course, never feels this way. He or she is perfectly willing to devote whatever time is necessary to maintain a beautiful lawn, and might even hope to achieve the best one in the neighborhood. These gardeners are certain that producing a fine lawn is the "right" way to landscape, and in many instances, such as on a country property, the "only" way to control wild spaces. Meanwhile, my husband and I go on blithely mowing about an acre of imperfect lawn almost every week during the growing season, and it serves our purposes well, indeed.

Our smaller areas of lawn receive basic care, but the largest part, our field lawn, planted originally by a farmer, is never watered, limed, raked, or fertilized. Perhaps meadow describes it best because it is full of wildflowers and clover, too. Unfortunately, the seeds tend to drift into adjacent garden beds where they must be eliminated, but to us, this effort is worthwhile rather than using herbicides on the meadow. During the warmer months of the year, except in the severest drought, merely mowing this field lawn—and leaving the grass clippings where they fall--results in a respectable green within the confines of our fenced-in garden.

We've surely come a long way from the manual care required for the closely cropped grass in the Emperor of China's palace gardens from 157 to 187 BC, and the turf carpets of the ancient Mayans, Persians and Romans, as well as lawns in Northern Europe dating back to the Middle Ages. Some of these lawns were not turfgrasses at all but low perennial plantings of chamomile, a favorite with royalty in Elizabethan England. These were carefully tended by hand to eliminate weeds. Throughout history, those who could afford them considered lawn keeping a cultural requirement similar to surrounding one's self with art or music.

Eventually, many types of grasses were tried to achieve a dense turf. Early groundskeepers depended on the labor of peons with hand cutting tools or grazing animals to keep their lawns low, fresh, and green. Tall grasses were cut with scythes. Imagine how difficult that must have been! What a blessing was the invention of the first mowing machine, very much like today's simplest reel mower. It first appeared in Gloucestershire, England, in 1830, and like almost all labor- saving devices, it soon became a necessity for those who cultivated a lawn.

What exactly is a lawn? According to "The American Heritage Dictionary of the English Language," it is a "plot of grass, usually tended or mowed around a residence, park, or an estate." To go further, one might say that a mown lawn is a living outdoor carpet of low green plants, pleasing in color, texture, fragrance, and of contrast in size and shape to taller ornamental plants. It is an open space that gives organization and definition to a garden. Furthermore, it can be viewed in a variety of ways—as a green plateau between sloping hills; an introduction to the home grounds; a space maintained for children's play; or merely a means of circulating throughout the rest of the garden.

Its principal value, if you are concerned with its environmental faults and benefits, is that it can be walked on—most of the time—as a simple pleasure. A paved path allows the gardener easy access to his plantings, but once you've stepped out onto grass, your feet will trod upon a living, growing domain that is a perfect accompaniment to your taller assembly of ornamentals.

From an aesthetic point of view, a newly greening lawn gives a great boost to our spirits. At about the time that migrating birds return from the south and spring peepers tweet in swampy areas, I hear another song—the awakening of our lawn. If you have a lawn, you, too, will hear it as it proclaims in its own clear voice: "It is spring!" As we move our activities outdoors, the well-established lawn on older properties can usually withstand whatever wear and tear is necessary.

Those who disapprove of lawns complain of environmental costs such as: mowers cut into precious gasoline reserves; lawn care irrigation leaves behind a depletion of aquifers; excessive fertilizer and herbicide runoffs clog our water supplies; and as a further indignity, gasoline powered mowers are too noisy. Should these arguments dissuade us from ever again cultivating a blade of grass? Consider the following:

Wherever thick carpets of lawn are grown, dust is dispersed into the atmosphere rather than into our houses, the main reason why many building codes will not permit home occupancy until a lawn is planted. Then, too, studies have indicated that unless you live very close to a busy highway, it is a combination of trees, shrubs, and grasses that does a satisfactory job of abating excessive noises. Through the transpiration of their foliage, turf-grasses also dissipate high levels of radiant heat into the atmosphere, thus saving the energy requirements of excessive air conditioning.

For the gardener, it is also comforting to know that as a lawn grows, many fine roots and other plant tissues are constantly decaying, thus improving the soil below it with this organic matter. Those who want to cultivate a vegetable garden could do no better than by using an area that was formerly thick sod.

A garden in rough terrain, or a garden where rainfall is always sparse, may not be able to support a bed of turfgrasses, but many gardens really depend on them for a mud-free passage from one corner of the property to the next. Other groundcovers will also help to disperse dust, abate noise and glare, and act as air conditioners, but in most cases, turf-grasses will probably do these jobs better.

To keep these lawns growing adequately as well as to control an excessive amount of time spent in maintenance, what we really need is a sensible approach to watering and fertilizing. Is it absolutely necessary, in every situation, to regularly apply lime, weed kill-ers, fungicides, fertilizers, and to regularly water, dethatch and rake? The answer is yes, if you are seeking perfection, but to grow a moderately successful lawn, you might be able to forego the constancy of some of these chores. Nevertheless, of all the elements necessary to its survival, the most important is a sufficient water supply.

Where rainfall is adequate, an established lawn will grow even without applying a great deal of fertilizer. Yet, I have observed that it is the exceptional gardener who knows the average yearly amount of precipitation that occurs in his own area. For example, in New York City, according to the New York Times Almanac, the public can expect a count of 44.12" annually. At my home, in northwestern New Jersey, a plentiful 51" of rainfall per year is normal. Unfortunately, normal is not always. One year recently, mid-summer meant a four week drought. Here, and in quite a few other Eastern seaboard states, this was preceded by a snowless winter that left area reservoirs with a serious water shortage. No one can be sure whether or not this is a trend caused by global warning, but when a temporary state of crisis hits us, this is no cause to rip out all our lawns because:

The following year, these states were deluged for weeks and weeks with almost unceas-ing rainfall (the year of the super lawn!) You, the renovating gardener, will rejoice when there is bountiful precipitation, and when drought is expected, learn how to cope by heed-ing the experts. Here are some of their suggestions:

Whether you have an in-the-ground sprinkler system or you depend on hoses and temporary sprinkler heads, adjust the use to days when your lawn is temporarily dry, and then soak deeply. Early morning, when the winds are calmest and temperatures are at their lowest, is probably the best time to irrigate. When you mow, try not to remove more than one third (about 1") of the top of each blade of grass and also, allow the clippings to remain where they fall rather than collecting and removing them. You'll find that the decaying clippings, if chopped fine, will return a good deal of organic nutrients to the soil, and thus, lessen the need for chemical fertilizers.

If you are really feeling guilty about using too much water, pursue additional conservation methods such as restricting superfluous water in your toilet; using the "gray water" left over from household chores by redirecting the water pipes into your garden; collecting rain water for newly planted ornamentals and potted plants; and covering outdoor swimming pools on hot, dry days or any time that they are not being used such as when you leave home for a trip. Rain barrels can be useful too, but they need careful monitoring to be sure that they don't become breeding places for mosquitoes. When necessary, any or all of these methods should help preserve a water supply.

In areas where there is minimal rainfall, Xeriscaping seems to make good sense. This means using drought tolerant groundcovers instead of most turfgrasses. Unfortunately, not all gardeners who grow these plants can accustom themselves to restricted irrigation, thus defeating their very purpose. In other areas, where rainfall is usually adequate, many new strains of turfgrasses, especially Kentucky Bluegrass in combination with some of the hardy latest rye grass strains, are said to be amazingly resilient to the occasional drought.

If you live in an area which only occasionally suffers a long, dry period in mid-summer, your lawns will simply cease growing during that time without being irrigated. Is this so terrible when compared with the enjoyment of your lawn at other times of the year? We should not expect to keep a lawn verdant during a drought. This loss of color is as natural as leaves dropping off deciduous trees in autumn. If you are interested in having a low maintenance lawn, adjust your thinking to accept occasional periods of dormancy. It is during this time that you had best "keep off the grass!" because foot traffic can further dehydrate struggling grasses.

Those who question the use of herbicides should certainly avoid them entirely during the heat of the summer or whenever droughty conditions prevail. They tend to stress grasses even further. Increasingly, "weed and feed" has been promulgated as the one and only way to treat a lawn under normal conditions. A better idea, from an environmental point of view, is to feed frequently with shredded grass clippings and to hand dig any weeds that really bother you—if they are not too numerous. Use a trowel with a long, sharp, tapered blade and if possible, work when the soil is at least slightly moist. If it is bone dry when this ambition hits you, then you'll first need to water each weed patch deeply. Sometimes, the dew of early morning will be enough to moisten the soil a bit and make the job easier. Under normal conditions, if you must use an herbicide, apply it directly on weeds that you want to eliminate rather than on the entire lawn. In spring, reseed bare spots early with fast germinating ryegrass remembering to keep the area damp until the seed germinates. The best time of all for germination without too much weed growth is in early fall. This is the season to go over the area with more permanent seed mixtures.

When it comes to fertilizing, gardeners should learn to "go with the tide." The tide, in turfgrass growth, is when grass plants can best use extra nutrients, and that is either in early spring or late fall. To avoid excessive fertilizer run-off, especially from those heavily composed of nitrogen, apply time-release organic fertilizers. Too much nitrogen is what causes quick growth that leads to more mowing. If the time- release does not produce enough green to satisfy you, it can be applied every few months of the growing season. Once you get your lawn into a reasonably decent shape, you can then return to once-a-season fertilization.

Sometimes, part of the problem is high acidity in the soil. If you suspect that this is the case, you should bring a soil sample to your agricultural agent to be tested and he or she will tell you if a correction with the addition of lime is needed. Do not be surprised, however, if you discover that adding lime is not necessary because a proper application can last three to five years, and most lawn grasses will grow in as wide a PH range as 5.5 to 7.5 At the same time, your agent should be able to suggest a particular type of fertilizer that will correct short-term nutrient deficiencies.

If you, the renovating gardener, think that your old lawn is rather shabby and you are debating with yourself what to do with it, examine it carefully to determine whether the greater mass is satisfactory. If so, then you have something to start with, much easier than removing the old and installing the new—although old sod makes excellent compost. If more than a third of the grass is undesirable, it will probably require too much work to improve the whole and it might be best to tear it out, add topsoil below the surface, and then sod or reseed.

Establishing an entirely new lawn is a process far too lengthy to describe here, but it does have one great advantage. In recent years, there has been a marked improvement in lawn seed. A broad range of superior blends is now available that is more resistant to disease, needs less mowing, and/or is more tolerant of variations in temperature and rainfall. New "smart" strains for a variety of climates are being introduced by specialty seed companies. Some contain a fungus that repels insects; others are an exceedingly dark green color which cuts down on the need for fertilizer. Still others do well on home lawns that drift from sun to shade. Better kinds of fescues for shady areas are also available now for more carefree cultivation. However, patching your existing lawn with new kinds of seed might not be a good idea if you are a fussy lawnkeeper since the result could be drastically different than what you have and create an uneven appearance. In case you're uncertain as to the best seed to buy for your particular situation, get in touch with the Turfgrass Resource Center in Rolling Meadows, IL, and they will answer your questions.

Most probably, if yours is a newly inherited lawn, you have no idea of the type or condition of the soil beneath it. That, of course, is the key to the lawn's renewable capacity especially in a drought. Why not take a spade and dig down 5" or so to determine whether the below-turf soil will be receptive to the nutrients that are needed? Heavy clay is great under a driveway, but as far as soil for a lawn is concerned, it prevents air and water from reaching grass roots. We readily appreciate sand on a beach, but under a lawn, water and nutrients flow quickly through and don't allow grass plants to absorb what they need. In either case, you might try a seasonally repeated light top-dressing with high quality compost or other amendments. It's a slow process, but gradually, the soil should become more friable. In turn, it will improve the quality of the existing grasses.

The lawns in our own country garden are not at all perfect. Low wildflowers amidst the grasses (I won't call them weeds) are abundant, but since our land is at the lowest point between surrounding hills, I can actually watch fluffy, silky-haired dandelion seeds floating down into our garden from above. To my regret, they creep into our ornamental beds and lawns. Mowing before the dandelions go to seed does help to prevent their spread. Appearing in our front lawn every spring are several types of wild violets, a low form of pussytoes and in a shady area, Quaker's ladies, also known as bluets, all of which we enjoy. The indiscriminate use of chemical herbicides here doesn't seem like a good idea here for two reasons: one is that we do not want to kill off these wildflowers, and two, we do not want to risk run-off and possible injury to the fish in our pond. Yet, our lawns, except where there is an invasion of an overly aggressive species, are quite satisfactory to us. Decisions such as this are what make every property unique. Maybe, when it comes to lawns, an attitude adjustment is needed most!

We use a slow release fertilizer every autumn to keep our front and back lawns growing reasonably well. An inexpensive, low-maintenance tool that does a good application job is a shoulder-carried, hand-cranked spreader that adjusts for the precise distribution of either pelleted or granular materials. It is particularly effective where there are slight rises or hills in the lawn. In this case, pushing a broadcast spreader sometimes requires great effort. The model hand-cranker that my husband prefers comes with a canvas bag which he finds far more comfortable against the body than a poly model. It gives a good, broad spread, and it makes the job quick and easy. For those who have minimum square feet to cover, a small, poly hand-cranker performs quite nicely and is readily available.

Organic matter in the form of grass clippings left by a mulching mower is a good source of lawn nutrition. Allowing the clippings to remain is a bit like making compost in place rather than in a separate area. The clippings must be shredded into small bits to rot quickly, but if you do not have a mulching mower, merely mowing over the lawn several times should do the trick. This saves a great deal of time that would otherwise be spent bagging and carting away the clippings.

Another thing that lowers maintenance time is mowing the lawn high and leaving about 2-3" of turf. Blades of grass cut too short run out of fertility rather quickly.

Many homeowners believe that lawn care is the most labor demanding garden chore. That has not been our experience. Some time ago, I read an article in a professional nurseryman's journal by a Dr. Don Williams, a horticultural professor at the University of Tennessee. Dr. Williams did a time study for the care of his 1.5 acre garden and determined that groundcovers, mulches, wildflowers, and other non-lawn planted areas are far more time consuming to maintain than turfgrass, and we agree. Our own situation at Frog Pond Farm is that with the proper equipment, we can mow our three sections of lawn in about two or three hours per week, sometimes less. This is just a drop in the bucket compared to all the other jobs required to keep our other plantings in good condition.

The most essential equipment we use on our property is the lawn tractor often used with an attached cart. We have three of them with one that is exceptional for its superb cutting ability. Another is used mostly for mulching and the third, for debris removal. Sometimes, two tractors are used for mowing at the same time. On any of them, the carts can be easily released or assembled, a great improvement over a wheelbarrow in large gardens where weeds and brush must be frequently removed.

On some properties, a riding mower, rather than a tractor, may be a good choice, especially if your lawn has a great many ins and outs, loops and curves.

Two major differences between riding mowers and tractors concern the engine placement and the tires. Riding mowers have the engine at the rear; tractors, at the front. Riders always have wide turf-tread tires so that they don't dig into the lawn and leave a mark. Our tractors also have turf-treads, but if you want to purchase one exclusively for rough, heavy duty mowing--places where the grass is allowed to grow quite tall--look for one that has bar-treads. All tractors are powerful workhorses with diversified uses.

Most mowers have detachable grass catchers, but these days, many types of machines cut the grass into small fragments producing finely cut mulch. For the good of your lawn, forget the catchers (except on those occasions when the grass has grown unusually high), and leave the clippings in place where they will soon decay and add nutrients to the soil.

A few years ago, my husband built a separate mulching attachment to shred autumn leaves. It can also be purchased, and is an unexcelled piece of equipment in gardens like Frog Pond Farm where fallen autumn leaves are exceedingly abundant. He places the machine in a cart where it is connected to the mowing apparatus. Beds are first raked or blown clear of heavy leaf accumulations which are then gathered into small piles on the lawn. When driving over the piles, the leaves are shredded and blown into the cart. They produce fabulous material which is returned to the beds for the winter.

All mowing machines, even those that cut easily in a tight radius, are easier to use when the loops and twists in the lawn are not too radical. When walking around your garden, search for these difficult-to-mow places and try to minimize them. When your lawn meets a wall or is at the top or bottom of a staircase, any place that you've previously been cutting with a hand tool, the mowing pattern can be simplified by installing an apron other than grass. For example, the steps leading down from our north facing patio are met, on each side, with rock retaining walls, each fronted with a narrow border planting. I connected the borders and then embedded large, flat stepping stones in the landing platform. Between the stones I planted low growing native partridge berries *(Mitchella repens)* which do well in this shady spot even with a bit of foot traffic. If it were a sunny area, I would probably use one of the creeping thymes. Mowing in front of the continuous borders is now a breeze.

All in all, a great many homeowners are overly concerned with lawn perfection rather than garden perfection. If you have traveled to see some of the world's greatest gardens, then I think you'll agree that maintaining a perfect lawn is not always a priority with all groundskeepers. It is the beauty of their gardens as a whole that gives them their distinctive character.

If you do your own mowing, be alert to any obstacles in your path. Side-discharge mowers can eject small stones or other objects that might injure bystanders. When your path is clear, relax a bit because driving a tractor or a riding mower can be a lot of fun. There's that attitude adjustment again.

CHAPTER XII
TO KEEP OR GRUB THAT FLOWERING SHRUB

Natalia Petrsanyte

CHAPTER XII
To Keep Or Grub That Flowering Shrub

Let us suppose that you've only recently settled on an older property with an aged lilac. Don't you feel awe-struck by its exuberant seasonal display of fragrant panicles? Or perhaps you were the one who planted this charmer long ago, and through the years, observed it reach its full potential. But if your older landscape includes many other flowering shrubs, the basic components of every garden, some might not have aged gracefully. If so, which should you grub? Better still, think of this as an opportunity to add the new and exciting to your garden.

We know that many new cultivars are introduced every year. Glowing catalogue descriptions and photographs tempt us to replace the old-fashioned with the up-to-date. Some of today's newest introductions have the ability to bloom longer, or are shorter in stature, or exhibit more disease resistance, or have flowers of a color never seen before, or carry foliage that is distinctively different, perhaps variegated. You ponder whether or not they can compete with those fine old shrubs that have faithfully fulfilled their destinies regardless of drought or torrential rains or freak temperature extremes. Shrubs that have proven their merit set them apart by having already weathered the worst and best of times while bringing untold beauty to your garden. However, beauty is not the only consideration when we decide which shrubs we should retain and which to replace.

Thirty years ago, my husband and I planted two Korean lilacs *Syringa meyeri* ('Palibin', syn. 'Palibiniana) on the little hill by our back path. These cultivars were described as charming because of their dwarf stature and bloom time far later than most other lilacs. We could expect, the references told us, a mature height of from 4-6', but often those figures refer to a size at ten years. Here were the lilacs, thirty years later, lovely and mildew free, which is a plus with these shrubs. But when they both topped 10' in height and girth, it was disappointing. Two were too much for this site! What really alarmed us was when the branches of one of them pushed against my upper story greenhouse and threatened to break the glass. We decided to retain one but the worst offender had to go. After its removal, the little hillside planting looked far less crowded and more in scale. Nurseries still offer this lilac, a most worthy plant, but like many of us mortals, excess weight and spread are sometimes part of the aging process.

Decisions, Decisions:

Examine your aging shrubs with eagle eyes and a questioning mind. Look at each plant from many angles before deciding whether its placement adds or detracts from the space that it occupies. If the shrub has grown too large for its site, think about replacing it with compact forms of cotoneasters, hydrangeas, spiraeas, rhododendrons, or other dwarf shrubs. Competition for a growing area can sometimes come from unexpected sources. Recently, I realized that some of my low-growing azaleas were being choked out of their new growth by the slow-to-ripen foliage of narcissus bulbs! In another place, a row of the lovely 4' tall *Azalea* 'Corsage" had spread 9' in width and now threatens to overwhelm our rear path. Transplanting them elsewhere is not an option for us given their enormous girth, and tip pruning only encourages more growth, One day—when I can get up enough courage—I'll cut down to soil level some of the branches close to the walk. At best, this is only a temporary solution to a knotty problem.

Old lilacs benefit from having a third of their total size pruned away every so often to encourage bloom on new wood, so you must decide if you are willing to do this. Then, determine whether your other sun-loving shrubs are getting enough light for splendid flower production without forever having to cut back adjacent trees or other impeding vegetation.

Overgrowth may not be one of your shrub problems. Perhaps the specimen in question is forever in need of being sprayed to combat rust, mildew, scale, or attacks by other damaging insects. If so, then now might be the time to grub it out and lessen one of your maintenance headaches.

Sometimes a shrub ceases to be attractive because its branches are no longer dense and full from top to bottom which is what you want if it's part of a screen planting. Careful pruning can sometimes correct this, but starting from scratch with fresh, young specimens is often a quicker and more satisfactory solution.

There is yet another thing for you to consider. It involves the overuse of certain shrubs, plants that are so common and so lacking in splendid year-long qualities that they might well be replaced. Brash, golden yellow old species forsythias are among them. If these shrubs were planted in poor soil, are serving a purpose as a vigorous screen planting, and if you simply love them, by all means keep them. You should know that certain new forsythia cultivars are of a more delicate shade of gold. There are also some true dwarfs, such as *Forsythia viridissima bronxensis*, that might make a splendid groundcover if that is what you need. Yet, do remember that when out of bloom, the foliage of most forsythias is nothing much to boast about.

If the only reason you are loathe to part with your old forsythias is because they serve as a welcoming harbinger of spring, then you might better consider several other deciduous shrubs that also bloom early. Among these are the andromedas (*Pieris japonica*), the native spicebush *(Lindera benzoin)*, Cornelian cherry *(Cornus mas)*, the February daphne *(Daphne mezereum)*, the fragrant winter-hazel *(Corylopsis glabrescens)*, the Korean azalea *(Rhododendron mucronulatum)*, and the pinkshell azalea *(Rhododendron vaseyi)*. All of these, and many more, are species that are not quite as omnipresent in everybody's back yard.

In April, May, and June, there are many hardy flowering shrubs that can be counted on to add lovely fragrance and/or color to a garden. Wherever the soil is acidic, ericaceous plants, such as rhododendrons and azaleas, cannot be beat for filling partially shady niches. Many species or cultivars of shrub roses, spiraeas, cotoneasters, deutzias, fothergillas, and viburnums are prime subjects for sun-bathed areas. Perhaps what you really desire are shrubs with an exceptionally long period of bloom. Or maybe you'd like to see some that have a shape and habit that is a little unusual and would just fit that difficult area of yours. Or this may be the time to add at least one shrub with variegated foliage such as the *Forsythia viridissima koreana* 'Kumson' from Korea with dark green leaves accented with silver and yellow venations.

If your soils and climate permit, and you can grow many kinds of evergreen rhododendrons, consider yourself fortunate. With magnificent foliage and flowers, they are among the most noble of plants. Yet, with the arrival of summer, where have all their blossoms gone? To be sure, there are some species in this genus, such as *Rhododendron viscosum*, that are at their blooming best in midsummer, but the majority of ericacae are finished blooming by the end of June. Your garden won't let you down in July, August, and September if you go out of your way to locate and plant other shrubs that are at their best in hot weather. You might try four of my favorites: *Aesculus parviflora*, the bottle-brush buckeye, with graceful white candles and interesting, brown seed capsules; *Clethra alnifolia rosea*, the summersweet, with prolific racemes of light pink flowers that are cherished by butterflies; *Itea virginica* 'Henry's Garnet,' the sweetspire, with slightly fragrant white flowers; and *Heptacodium miconoides*, the Seven-sons plant, tall and floriferous, blooming in late August, early September with additional color from its red sepals that last until autumn. These shrubs may not be available in the average garden center, so you'll probably need to purchase them farther afield. More and more, mail order specialty nurseries are offering exquisite cultivars of these shrubs. It is well worth seeking them out.

For high season interest, I have found, there is another group of plants that is difficult to categorize. Some call them subshrubs; others, woody perennials, plants that should be cut down to grade every spring. *Santolina chamaecyparissus*, the silvery-white leafed lavender cotton, is one of them, growing from 1-2'. Another, *Teucrium chamaedrys*, grows to about the same height. The later has small, oval leaves and mid-summer purple flowers. I enjoyed them both in my former garden, but alas, here in Zone 5, they are not quite hardy enough to be called permanent shrubs.

If you have enough space for a broad, 6' tall, late summer blooming subshrub, *Lespedeza thunbergii* 'Gibralter', is terrific. This bush clover is completely dependable here for its late summer, early fall purple-pink flowers in great quantities. Unfortunately, its white flowered form, L.t. 'Albiflora', blooms a little too late for me and is sometimes cut down by an early frost, but it might all right in your garden.

Another subshrub that I recently planted is the Chinese indigo, *Indigofera kirilowii*, only growing to about 18" in height. Reputedly, its pink flowers bloom from June through September on pea-like foliage, but promises, promises from many garden catalogues must be tested to be found true, so I will wait and see. This indigo is described as an everblooming, midsummer subshrub which should certainly appeal to those who seek other than spring flowering shrubs.

We have all read a great deal about planting perennials to coordinate with existing shrubs, but in the older garden, if you want to ease your maintenance, you can also do it the other way around. If you have a border of tall growing perennials fronted by lower growers, the later needing replacement, you might do so by planting small or moderate sized shrubs. Dwarf forms of fothergilla, spiraea, deutzia, and hydrangea might fit the bill. Daphnes are spectacular, but some species tend to be short lived unless you can give them extra special attention.

Size, shape, and hardiness, are, of course, the important features governing our choices In addition to these factors, you might inquire about drainage requirements, PH preference (acidity or alkalinity), and ease of maintenance for shrubs that you're considering. Does this sound like you must spend more time studying than gardening? Not so. This kind of information is readily available to anyone willing to spend a little time on the Internet or in a public library.

For the Birds:

As you renovate your old garden, you will certainly not want to remove every healthy shrub that sports ample seed and fruit for songbirds. It has been my experience that the more small birds in my landscape, the fewer problems I have with insect mutilated plants.

Birds bring more than color and sweet song to the garden. According to the Garden Club of America's Conservation Committee, brown thrashers can eat 6,180 insects in a day, Baltimore orioles consume over 17 hairy caterpillars in a minute, and one little swallow can devour 1000 leafhoppers in twelve hours. And that's just the tip of the iceberg. I wonder how much toxic spray a gardener would have to apply to rid our gardens of damaging insects compared to a flock of tree swallows and their huge appetites! Whenever possible, let birds solve your worst insect problems.

When rearranging your garden, it's not a bad idea to give preference to ornamental fruiting plants, either introduced or natives. If you have a few shrubs with edible fruit that you enjoy and save for yourself, protect them with netting. It's worth going to this extra trouble where the bird population is heavy. We grow a dozen or so blueberry shrubs within a house-like structure covered with netting. The harvest is so abundant that when we have picked our fill, we remove the overhead netting and let the birds clean up the rest.

Among my favorite shrubs with lovely ornamental fruit are the chokeberry (*Aronia arbutifolia* 'Brilliantissima') with red berries; the Japanese beauty-berry (*Callicarpa japonica*) with purple fruit; the silky dogwood shrub *(Cornus amomum)* with blue fruit; winterberries *(Ilex verticillata)* with scarlet or salmon fruit; the Indian currant *(Symphoricarpos orbiculatus)* with rose-pink fruit, the American cranberry *(Viburnum trilobum)* with orange-red fruit as well as the Asian *Viburnum dilatatum* with red berries that remain on into winter.. and there are others. Very interesting, also, is *Viburnum plicatum* 'Watanabe' (also listed as 'Fujiyanensis'), an 8-10' rather slim upright. This delightful viburnum blooms on and off all summer and also bears great quantities of scarlet fruit in midsummer. By early September, feasting birds will end its berry display, but observing their enjoyment is worth the loss. As you can readily see, a fine selection of shrubs can be as varied and as colorful as a border of perennials. Remember, though, that some shrubs will need both a male and females to produce a crop of berries.

On the rear bank of the dam of our pond, the staghorn sumac *(Rhus typhina)* seeded itself into a colony. They became one of nature's pleasant accidents since their laciniated leaves, in great contrast to other foliage around them, reflect so beautifully in the pond waters. Over 17 bird species relish their unusual fruit. The soil on this bank is poor and dry and the sumacs did not seem to spread to other areas so their somewhat invasive habit was no problem here. These are the kind of decisions that every gardener should make while keeping a watchful eye on the consequences of his actions.

On a good sized property, don't be in a hurry to remove every shrub or tree that is dead or dying of old age. Many birds covet the hollows in dead wood and use them for shelter in bad weather. But if that shrub is well within your most common line-of-sight, and it looks frightful in its decline, it might be better to grub it. Do so after it has lost its leaves in autumn to avoid the possibility of destroying a bird's temporary home.

Runaways:

"Plant only natives," say some, intimating that exotic plants have no place in our gardens. Does this mean that you, the renovating gardener, should destroy any shrub (or other plant) that originated in another country? It is a topic on which much has been written, sometimes controversially, but always with great fervor. It is true that runaway damage can occur when an imported plant is too happy in its new environment and becomes a noxious invader. In its homeland, such a plant behaves itself, but whatever kept it in check there is missing in its new country. Among these invaders are not only shrubs but also certain trees, vines, grasses, ferns, and perennials. Perhaps you, too, have been battling introduced runaways that threaten to overtake your most precious plants. Where completely ignored, as in an abandoned lot, they can strangle all other vegetation. According to a 1999 article in Audubon magazine, at least 400 alien plants in the U.S. are considered dangerously destructive to our environment. The problem with recommending the garden planting of only natives is that our country is not without its own indigenous thugs.

Besides the fox grape which I discussed earlier, a vine that often strangles host trees, the native Virginia creeper *(Parthenocissus quinquefolia)* is also a problem. It is a vine with dramatic red autumn foliage, but in many eastern U.S. locations, it seeds far too prolifically to be welcome into gardens. And then there is that southern and Midwestern tree, the black locust *(Robinia pseudoacacia)*. It has spread to every state in the union (except Arizona) and should also be called a runaway. There are others.

It is quite disturbing for me to read the words of those who insist that we plant only ornamentals native to our area or to some place in our country. One glance at our magnificent Korean dogwood *(Cornus kousa)* in bloom would convince you that the country of Korea is a splendid place for locating outstanding plants. To disallow its entry, or any other foreign introduction, would be to deprive us of some of the most beautiful ornamentals on the face of the earth. Imagine how wretched our gardens would be without evergreen hollies, Asian rhododendrons and azaleas, andromedas, Japanese maples, lilacs, some of our best viburnums, weigelas—the list goes on and on. One authority states that about 90 per cent of our landscape ornamentals would be relegated to "forbidden" status if we were allowed to plant only natives. Some conservationists argue that indigenous shrubs attract wildlife, intimating that species introduced from other countries do not. It is inconceivable to me that a bird would reject the copious fruits of the Asian Linden viburnum (*Viburnum dilatatum*), the European cranberry *(Viburnum opulus)*, or the Japanese Wright viburnum *(Viburnum wrightii)*, finding only the native berries edible. Fruiting plants of many kinds, both native and introduced, feed songbird populations.

One native shrub or small tree with which I am all too familiar is that ubiquitous East Coast conifer, the winter gloomy American red cedar (*Juniperus virginiana*) Yet, many horticulturists recommend this plant for landscaping, a species that seeds about all too freely. When it appears in my garden, I dig it out. True, the seeds of this conifer are cherished by a host of birds, but many pines, spruce, and hemlocks also produce cone-bearing seed that they enjoy.

Even in its improved cultivar forms, I would ban the red cedar; it is an alternate host of cedar apple rust which can seriously mar the foliage of both shrubby and tree stature crabapples. Sooner or later, if these conifers are within three miles of ornamental barberries or crabapples, the rust disease will probably spread to them. It took twenty-five years before a neighborhood's red cedars began to damage the foliage of our crabs, and now, these flowering trees must be sprayed with a fungicide several times each spring. There is nothing I can do to remove my neighbor's offending conifers, but those who recommend the species should reexamine their thinking, and I opt to rid them from all our gardens. Wherever possible, they should also be removed from fields where they have seeded. Obviously, those with commercial apple orchards would also benefit. With one less spray for them to contend with, the cost of these fruit might even be reduced! The Rocky Mountain juniper *(Juniperus scopulorum)* is also suspect as a host for this disease.

Some shrubs, of course, are grown specifically for their root-running capacity within a given area, but if they do not run about indiscriminately, can serve a purpose in a difficult situation. I am thinking of the Eastern American summersweet *(Clethra alnifolia)* that has increased by underground stems on a moist, shady bank above our pond. Planted years ago, the clethras have nicely prevented the slope from eroding.

Yet true thug plants, whether native or introduced from abroad, should be avoided like the plague. Explorers, botanists, and plant breeders have brought, and continue to bring us a wealth of beauty from many parts of the world. Knowledgeable gardeners would be foolish to ignore their contributions unconditionally. Certainly not all importations are invasive; if this were so, then corn and wheat, both of which originated outside of the U.S., would have spread to almost every open part of our country. The same might be said of certain other living things, too, such as the three kinds of beneficial earthworms introduced inadvertently from abroad, species of worms that were not present in our soils before the arrival of Europeans, and that have proven to be indispensable as soil improvers. Nevertheless, there is a price to pay for any living thing that is not thoroughly tested for possible runaway tendencies.

A typical offender in much of the East coast is the Japanese *Rosa multiflora* which gives me my biggest headache. It dots the fields and open spaces all around me. Yet I would not be surprised to find that some gardeners actually encourage more growth with applications of fertilizer. "Here is a pretty rose that grows without any bother," they tell themselves. True, when in bloom, its fragrant white flowers are enormously appealing. Birds must think they are in paradise when they come upon a stand of fruiting multifloras. They greedily devour its prolific fall and winter fruit, and then evacuate the seeds whenever and wherever. Seed germination must be phenomenal, the reason these roses have spread so viciously everywhere there is a bit of sun. If they have entered your garden, and you decide to eliminate them, you will have to contend with their sharp thorns and huge root systems.

I have spent a good portion of my life uprooting the seedlings of this rose as they appear in my garden and am now hoping to eliminate it and other unwanted invaders from the fringes of our property. Biologists are now experimenting with a variety of promising natural controls, but as of this writing, these methods (a disease-producing pathogen, a native mite, and a seed-destroying wasp) may also infect ornamental roses, surely not an acceptable situation. Hopefully, if you are reading this some years hence, these scientists will have solved the problem.

In recent years, *Euonymous alatus*, the burning bush, has also become invasive here. It is a species that I planted myself, in its dwarf form compacta, for its spectacular fall foliage. Its seedlings are tough little monsters to dislodge by hand as I discovered when weeding my myrtle beds. A better choice these days might be the native American *Rhus copallina*, a slow growing sumac with shiny leaves and brilliant scarlet autumn foliage. Then, too, the countryside around us is surrounded by old-field honeysuckles (*Lonicera japonica*), plants that often strangle the growth of handsome native trees. Now I read that some Japanese originated forms of spiraea and the Asian Russian olive (*Elaeagnus angustifolius)* have also become invasive for some of us. While working in your garden, you, too, may find yourself all too busy plucking out runaway plants. Weeding, of course, is always part of cultivating plants, for we must not expect a garden to be as sterile as a hospital room. Yet, every overly rampant invader should be treated as your garden's enemy.

And so we see that both exotics and native plants can have rapacious tendencies. Perhaps run-away competition is one of the reasons why the last two centuries have seen about 200 diverse North American native plant species become extinct. Thousands more are also being threatened. We lose many attractive, and possibly useful plants, for a variety of reasons, but the struggle for supremacy from overly aggressive species is one of them. On the other hand, consider this: perhaps just as many new species are evolving (without man's interference) along with extinctions. Who is to say that some will not become great garden additions? We might as well accept the fact that change is a part of life's cycle.

Evolutionary change may be easier to spot in animals. An area in New York State during the mid 1950s was the place where several dozen deer were discovered with snowy white coats. Their numbers have now grown into a sizeable herd. If deer were not such a forest and garden pest, such a change would be considered a splendid evolutionary addition to our wildlife.

When planting an unfamiliar new shrub, watch carefully to see whether or not it has invasive properties. When a rash of seedlings appear near a plant that you regard highly, think of this as a little miracle not an unwanted invasion. What we might watch for instead are plants that seed or root run indiscriminately at a distance from their original location. These are the ones that need eradication.

There are three important principles in dealing with the planting of native or and non-native shrubs. 1. Destroy both kinds of plants if they show signs of taking over space in several parts of your garden; 2. When purchasing newly introduced shrubs, choose those that are well known for their ability to thrive without growing out of control; and 3. Regardless of their place of origin, cherish those plants already on your property that are both handsome and particularly useful to bees, bats, butterflies, and birds without reproducing themselves all over your garden. Native or non-native should not be the issue.

Shrub Removal:

How to get rid of invasive shrubs in your garden? This case history might prove helpful:

We permitted two enormous clumps of the multiflora rose to grow on the north bank of our pond to discourage deer from entering our garden. What a mistake! Their seedlings sprouted everywhere. When, at last, tight fencing was put in place to deter the deer, we decided to remove these roses, a daunting task because of their enormous height, width, and sharp thorns. First, we used a gasoline-powered hedge trimmer to cut four or five feet off the upper branches. Then, reaching lower and heavier parts, we used tree loppers to remove as much as possible. The job was completed with a chain saw that cut the trunks flush with the ground. This was no job for pruning shears because of the thorns and thick stems. It required us to wear long-sleeved shirts, eye shields, and gloves, the latter which I rarely use in gardening. It was necessary to protect our eyes because the rose's flexible stems flap in the slightest breeze and jump out at you. Three people worked on this tedious job for over thirty hours. Nonetheless, at long last, it was a "done deal."

Now we were faced with a great deal of debris. The safest approach would have been to burn the entire tangle to avoid the possible germination of any seed, but open fires are not permitted in New Jersey. Instead, we hauled the entire mess off to our brush pile. Such piles, incidentally, are shelterbelts for many birds during inclement weather so if you have a place for one that is not too conspicuous, it will serve a good purpose. However, this is not the best way to deal with *Rosa multiflora*! We need government cooperation to allow the burning of invasive and disease ridden plant materials if we are ever to rid ourselves of this plague. If your property is not large enough for a substantial pile, you might consider employing a disposal service to haul the debris away. When this is necessary, my imagination takes me to the dump site, and I can clearly visualize it as sporting a forest of multifloras!

All our work on these roses was accomplished in late autumn, and since winter was closing in and the ground was freezing fast, we had to wait until the first reasonably dry day in early spring to dig out the remaining stumps with the bucket of our farm tractor. Since it is unlikely that most homeowners have such a tractor, you might try a different technique for reducing or eliminating stumps so that you will have room to plant substitute shrubs: As soon as possible after the shrub or tree is cut down to its base, use a paint brush dipped in one of three herbicides; glyphosate, dicamba, or ammonium sulfate. As you bring it to the stump, be very careful not to drip herbicide onto grass or any other plant that may be in the way. They are non-selective killers. Also, you might drill shallow holes into the stump and fill them with herbicide from an eyedropper. This technique works best with fresh stumps, but if any time has elapsed since the trunk was severed, try to cut the stump as low into the soil as possible before applying the herbicide.

Broadleafs:

If you asked me to name one of my favorite shrubs, I'd probably tell you that it is the bushy, moderate height, king protea *(Protea cynaroides)* from South Africa, a shrub with gorgeous leathery leaves and large, long lasting blooms of a color and form so exquisite that it defies a brief description. Alas, such a plant cannot, of course, be grown in my most American gardens (or even in a sheltering greenhouse) because it doesn't thrive in our soils and climates. Rather than coveting the impossible, we should all appreciate what we can easily grow. The soils here at Frog Pond Farm are slightly acidic and although winter temperatures have dropped to as low as –17 degrees F. and summer highs often soar to highs of 95 degrees F., many kinds of broadleaf evergreens have survived, even flourished, when properly sited. I would hate to be without our many semi-evergreen azaleas which are the backbone of our garden, or the many hybrid rhododendrons specifically bred to take climatic extremes. If you, too, have variable conditions, you might try Gable and Kaempferi azaleas. Other azaleas that do particularly well here are the Robin Hills, the species nakaharae, and satsuki azaleas. Where hardy, and also very satisfactory in a woodland setting, are mountain laurels *(Kalmia latifolia)* and drooping leucothoe *(Leucothoe fontanesiana)*, the latter useful in a variety of settings including those that are moderately moist.

If you have newly arrived at a property where the climate is quite harsh, yet you find that your landscape contains a great many different kinds of azaleas and rhododendrons, then you should know that some of them might have been slightly tender when they were planted. It is altogether possible that these were lightly covered with burlap the first few winters after planting, and that eventually they were uncovered as they became acclimatized to the existing conditions. Unlike most of us human beings, well grown azaleas and rhododendrons seem to grow hardier with each passing year.

In Zone 4, you might have to forego planting many of these broadleafs and choose, instead, deciduous Ericaceae. Fortunately, quite a few (although not all) of these azaleas and rhododendron will take fairly low temperatures. Here, at Frog Pond Farm, one of the most prized of all my shrubs is the native pinxter-bloom *(Rhododendron periclymenoides)*. Also called the wild honeysuckle, its pale pink blooms appear in unbelievable profusion each year. Sadly, only one of the original still exists here; the others were inadvertently destroyed in an early clearance of our hedgerow. And so, tread lightly if you should come across indigenous shrubs on your property that you are unable to quickly identify.

Above, I've only mentioned some of the many deciduous shrubs that I've planted throughout the years, but many a nursery specializes in others that are also handsome and dependable. As you can readily see, there is no longer any need to spend an endless amount of time shaping a formal hedge when the perfectly formed shrub is there somewhere—one that does not need extensive pruning.

Pruning:

Even in the naturalistic garden, at one time or another, almost every shrub will need some pruning. Here is a brief review of the why and how-to:

Pruning is especially beneficial to old shrubs that have lost their youthful vigor. It stimulates growth points into action. A shrub that has formed a multitude of canes from the base will flower far better if some of those canes are removed in early spring; some modern roses, blueberries, viburnums, and flowering quince are just a few plants that should respond well. If they might look too desecrated when this is accomplished in one season, do it over a period of several years taking off only a portion of the shrub each time instead of all at once. Other shrubs can be cut close to the ground every early spring; buddlejas and lespedezas are among them. Shrubs such as *Cornus sericea*, grown mostly for their dark red stems in winter, should be cut down almost to the ground every season because it is their fresh new growth that is the most colorful. Then there are others that have gotten leggy or completely out of balance. They would benefit by being cut back to a foot from grade level. This may be the case with some of your old mountain laurels *(Kalmia)* and large-leafed rhododendrons. It is amazing how these sturdy broadleafs slowly grow back from barren-looking stubs. Meanwhile, if they are in a prominent place, transplant them temporarily to a nursery area.

Spring flowering shrubs that bloom on wood formed the previous season should be pruned after their flower display. Summer flowering shrubs that bloom on wood formed at that season can be pruned in winter or early spring. This is what the references say but the problem is that it is sometimes difficult to tell if the plant blooms in late spring or early summer and which is old wood and which is new! Puzzled by this, you might ask your county extension agent about the particular shrub that you have in mind. The standard practice is to make your cut at an angle above a bud, but if you are unsure, again consult with the agent. The main point is to always cut out crossing or dead branches, whatever the season, and to use your pruning shears discriminatingly; thin, rather than shear, if you want to maintain the shrub's natural shape. Best of all, many young shrubs need little more than a slight touch with the pruning shears every so often.

More than once, I've cut off the stems that fed my desire for flowers; so if pruning has always been the bugaboo of your gardening life, take cheer in the fact that you are not alone. Almost every gardener, at one time or another, has made a pruning error and temporarily robbed his favorite flowering shrub of its form, bloom, or ability to thrive because of hurried pruning at the wrong time of the year or at the wrong place on the plant. When purchasing a new shrub, it is a plus to find a knowledgeable salesperson who is able to provide you with detailed information on how much pruning is required and the best time to accomplish this task. The more localized the information, the better, because climatic conditions differ from one place to another, and growth patterns may require different timing or techniques. Pruning practices in upper New York State, for example, such as cutting a shrub down to the ground each spring, might be destructive in California, and that is why one of your best sources of information is your local extension agent. If you are able to use a computer, there are many Internet sites that may be able to give you applicable information.

Deadheading (twisting off spent blooms) is a useful but time consuming process. I am not the only one who has noticed that after deadheading spent trusses on rhododendrons soon after bloom time, they usually produce a prodigious number of buds which turn into flowers the next spring. If you have the time, it's an easy task that has a nice reward. I've also tried this on mountain laurel, but having removed every new capsule formed one year after an unusually prolific flowering, not one bloom appeared the following year! It may be that I performed this task a little too late. Try it yourself as an interesting experiment.

If you have an inordinate number of mature rhodies, deadhead only your special favorites. They will all bloom anyway, although maybe not in great profusion. And if you have a large garden, don't fret that you were unable to prune all the older shrubs that needed it in one growing season. Unlike weeds, they'll wait at your convenience without any serious consequences

CHAPTER XIII
DOWN A TREE, UP A TREE

Natalia Petrianyk

CHAPTER XIII.
Down A Tree, Up A Tree

It's a common sight throughout the U.S.—the forlorn and empty look of a recently completed housing development swept clean of vegetation. Builders usually claim that this is necessary during the construction period. No matter how elegant the new dwellings, no matter how quickly landscapers rush to "green up" the site, removal of the original trees leaves a sad vacuum. Planting replacements as soon as possible is vital because, of all landscape elements, trees are the most conspicuous and permanent. The sooner they are established, the sooner each house setting begins its conversion into a welcoming new home.

It may very well be that because of your love for mature trees, you have chosen to purchase an older home. Or, if you've lived in this house for a long time, its trees are one of the reasons that you feel anchored to the place. Some of us form an emotional attachment to trees. The loss of a fine, aged specimen can be a traumatic experience. You, too, may have heard stories about soldiers returning home after years away at war to sadly discover that their favorite tree is gone forever.

Trees serve us in many ways. How much we appreciate an aged oak that cools us on a summer day, or a flowering dogwood, the perfect background for our photos, or those quivering aspen leaves that signal a coming storm. It is easy to see why mature trees are so greatly cherished by all of us who are sensitive to nature. Flourishing trees convey the message that home is a place of deep-rooted stability. But, as with all living things, time can also bring with it a host of unanticipated problems.

Case History: One sunny day, as I was having lunch in my kitchen, I heard a muffled, unfamiliar thump. Looking out, I saw that an enormous leafy branch from our callery pear had torn free from its trunk and lay on the lawn. In 1960, the U.S. Arboretum introduced this much-acclaimed ornamental cultivar of a species from China, *Pyrus calleryana* 'Bradford'. In 1975, we planted the 'Bradford' below our second story deck. At the time, I felt like I was a member of the horticultural avant-garde because here was something rather new and different, decidedly beautiful in flower, rich red foliage in autumn, and with a pyramidal habit perfectly suited to the space that I could provide. Little did I know that this species would become very popular all over the country, especially as a street tree. In the days to come, it was no longer considered a novelty. Nevertheless, I adored it.

Our 3-4' specimen grew quickly. In twenty-five years, it had reached a height of 30 to 40'. When walking out onto our deck in spring, I felt encased in a flowering mist, so prodigious and graceful were the tree's clusters of single white blooms. Birds nested in its branches, wind-chimes provided music for its swaying branches, and the leaves that followed the blossoms, free of insect damage, were among the earliest to appear of all the trees in our garden. I also prized it for being the very last of our trees to drop its beautiful foliage in autumn. Had I read further in the available literature, I might have known about this pear's serious problems.

Until the collapse of its first limb, I paid no attention to the large crotches between the tree's heavy branches that weakened its structure. A few years later, when a second branch broke off, we could see that more would soon follow, land on our roof, or cause other problems. The tree was self-destructing. My husband and I promptly chopped up the downed branches with loppers and a chain saw. Never before had we encountered such dense heavyweights as the pieces we carried off to our brush pile. Eventually, an arborist was called in who cut down the rest of the tree—at a considerable expense.

Then followed the decision-making process. Should we replace the 'Bradford' with another callery pear cultivar? There are many: P.c. 'Aristocrat,' 'Autumn Blaze,' 'Chanti-cleer', 'Redspire', some of which may or may not have the faults of our pear. In the end, we opted for another tree entirely, the Japanese tree lilac, *Syringa reticulata* 'Ivory Silk', which has many splendid attributes including profuse flowering, lovely fragrance, and interesting lenticels, the markings on the bark. My dilemma shows how important it is to thoroughly research the merits and faults of every existing tree you are thinking of planting. It is not like a suit or dress that you buy and return because it doesn't really fit or you've later decided is unattractive. Since many trees we plant might still exist long after we are gone, a careful choice should assure both you and your heirs that much pleasure will be derived from it well into the future.

Location, Location, Location:

When a tree struggles to grow, or even worse, looks as though it may not survive, chances are that neither insects nor drought, long periods of excessive heat, nor unexpected frost, are causing its flagging health. Your particular specimen may be the right species aesthetically but planted in the wrong place. Every gardener, sooner or later, learns the one essential fact about this art, and that is: Appearance and cultural needs must coincide. An artist, an interior designer, even a flower arranger, can move materials around until he or she has the desired visual effect, but when dealing with a living entity such as a tree, one cannot decide merely where it will look best. One must decide where it will grow best.

For example, the laceleaf Japanese maple is a very attractive small tree. It may seem to be the perfect tree, let us say, as the focal point of a dwarf conifer grouping, but if the site is open and breezy, its dissected foliage will look as though it has come through a meat grinder after every storm. These little maples are best planted in a wind protected area.

The right tree in the right location, given a reasonable amount of care in its initial planting and youthful years, should be able to surmount many difficulties and possibly live to a ripe old age. Longevity, of course, differs according to the species.

Here are some things to consider when dealing with an existing deciduous tree: If some of its leaves look droopy in midsummer, it may only be temporary distress caused by long, hot days without rainfall. A deep drink should help. However, when there is constant leaf drop from early spring through autumn, this may signal life foreshortened. Don't worry too much, though, if occasional branches fall to the ground. Think of this as Mother Nature doing her own pruning.

Perhaps the tree you worry about was thriving until damaged by a heavy, wet, snowstorm or a violent attack of hurricane-like winds. Examine it carefully and if approximately 50 percent of its limbs are still intact, the tree will probably recover. When a broken branch hangs limp and you cut it away, try to leave a collar at the place on the trunk where it was severed. Flush cuts invite decay. The collar area contains chemicals that will reduce the onset of disease although the larger the wound, the longer it will take to grow a healthy callus. The current thinking among arborists is to avoid applying tar, shellac, or other sealers to the cut. Leave it alone because nature can accomplish a great repair job all by itself.

A low, weeping cherry along our pond was a case in point. One summer day, a minor tornado ripped through here causing a tall, single trunked gray birch, 20' away from the cherry to fall through its center. The smaller tree is a prized specimen with branches cascading over the side of the pond. The weedy birch, all too common on our property, was of lesser consequence. Although the cherry lost few of its branches, about a quarter of its short trunk was badly wounded. I was certain that the tree would soon collapse entirely, but my husband urged me to wait and see. Happily, the wound healed sufficiently, and our cherry continues to thrive.

By all means, remove the broken branches on a tree when they are a major part of its structure. Even a badly damaged tree may make a full recovery if enough of the crown remains. Age can make a difference. The healthy, cherished sapling you planted not too long ago, like a child with amazing resiliency after an accident, should have a good chance of recovery from injuries if its dominant (terminal) leader is still intact.

If a tree grows too tall, it may sometimes be headed back a little with not too much difficulty. The main point in pruning is to remove each branch that interferes with another, and any that might be suffering from die-back.

Pruning old trees can be dangerous. Regardless of your skills, tall trees are far too dangerous to be tackled by the home gardener using a ladder or climbing onto a roof to repair storm damage. Every year, our newspapers are full of reported accidents, sometimes deaths, from fallen do-it-yourselfers. It is important to know when it is better to be a "don't do it yourself" gardener. Call in professional arborists to do the climbing.

The entire removal of large trees by certified experts can be quite expensive, but it is often a key part of renewing the vigor of older home landscapes. Sometimes, this is necessary if the tree was damaged by a storm, hurricane, or tornado. Unfortunately, your insurance company will not usually relieve you of the expense. Few people realize that homeowner's insurance will not cover this cost, which is categorized as an "Act of God." You may be jolted by some of the policy clauses such as: If one of your neighbor's trees collapses into your garden destroying some of your plantings, don't expect him or her to pay for any of the damages. Perversely, as it seems to me, some policies state: if one of your stricken trees falls onto your adjacent neighbor's property, he will be responsible for any damages and clean-up, not a happy situation for all concerned. However, if your neighbor has a failing tree near your boundary line, and some day, it may very well drop into your garden doing damage, it's to your benefit to have an arborist examine it and forecast its probable future. Then, you must advise your neighbor (by certified mail) of the problem. If the forecast comes true, you may be able to collect for damages. You may also be able to claim a deduction on your Federal Income Tax returns. It's an unpleasant business no matter how you figure it. Insurance policies by various companies may differ so if this troubles you, read the small print. The entire matter of "damage payment" only emphasizes the fact that when planting, it's important to choose a site where the new tree has adequate room. Give it a fighting chance to reach old age under the best possible conditions. Then, too, recognize that some trees weather storm damage better than others.

Choosing And Planting A New Tree:

If you want to replace a downed tree, think of it as an opportunity to demonstrate your growing design ability. Consider the tree planted in the middle of a lawn, surrounded by a thick bed of mulch. In such a situation, unless you have an exceptional mower, you've always needed extra time to cut the grass around it. Now, minimizing that time has become a priority with you. Why feel obligated to fill the same space with another tree? Possibly, you've gained a pleasing openness or you have exposed an unexpected view of your garden that is most attractive. By all means, plant a new tree, but it does not have to be in the exact spot that was formerly occupied.

From an aesthetic point of view, a small bed circling a young tree in the middle of a lawn always looks to me like one small fish in a large aquarium. A far more natural look is achieved by planting it within an extended side border, if that is possible. Then, apply the mulch, and, after it grows to a reasonable height and spread, fill the space below with shade loving groundcovers.

I've said this before, but it's worth repeating: If you've lost a new tree, the chances are that it was the wrong species for its location. Perhaps it was not hardy enough to endure an unusually cold winter or an exceptionally hot summer, nor was it able to cope with the wet spot in which it was planted. Additionally, insect or disease problems can terminate the life of a tree. Browsing through a professional nurseryman's journal recently, I compiled a list of current debilitating tree problems. There are so many possibilities that it's enough to cause a gardener to become a tree hypochondriac. Attacking ornamental trees somewhere in the U.S. early in this 21st century are: gypsy moths, lace bugs, longhorned beetles, woolly adelgid, Dutch elm disease, Asian ambrosia beetle, dogwood anthracnose, sudden oak death, two-spotted spider mite, lilac borer, pine moths, birch leafminer, and spruce needle miner. There are many more but this is no time to hang up your shovel. Not all species have severe problems. Maybe the variety of afflictions isn't so surprising if you consider the long list of maladies that can occur in humans. Can doesn't mean will.

When selecting a new tree for your garden, you should ascertain how probable is the "can." Consult with your county's agricultural extension service and ask them whether or not the disease or insect infestation in question is prevalent in your area. It is altogether possible that where you live, the tree that you have in mind does not have a problem. In my own area, I often wonder why some local nurseryman still offer for sale the Austrian pine *(Pinus nigra)* when now, the diplodea tip blight mars its beauty. The last thing that you want to do is garden with a spray container of chemicals which may not even help.

Having decided which tree you'd like to introduce to your garden, the next step is determining how large the new specimen should be when purchased. Although not everyone will agree, experience has taught me that do-it-yourself homeowners should avoid buying very large trees. To me, they are usually a waste of time and money. Studies show very slow root growth in large, transplanted specimens and thus, the critical period of establishment can take two, three, or even four years. In the heat of summer, a good sized root ball needs an enormous amount of water. Hired crews who plant such trees know that part of their maintenance responsibilities is keeping up with deep watering unless rain does the job. Big trees, of course, do give more of an immediate effect, and sometimes, they are almost a necessity. But if you are the caretaker, even a conscientious gardener, sooner or later you might forget the watering at a critical time. In any case, I've seen that trees 6 to 8' tall are easier to irrigate and faster growing. They will probably catch up with large transplants in a short period of time. Even if you can afford to have a large tree planted for you, chances are that you will be well ahead of the game if you select one that is smaller and youthfully vigorous.

For trees less than 3 or 4' tall, a mail order catalogue is a good source for potted trees, and from some firms, you'll get an enormous choice. Also, early in the growing season, young deciduous trees are sometimes offered bare root, without soil around the roots. Even if the cost is reasonable, I'm not particularly happy with these offerings because, all too often, a great many branches and roots must be pruned back before planting, and there goes the advantage of the reasonable price. Additionally, if you intend to plant in spring but the soils in your area are slow to dry, you may have to wait before digging the new hole. Meanwhile, bare root trees have put out their leaves, a situation common in my garden and not to be recommended.

Many retail nurserymen today are growing their trees (and shrubs) in containers. While this makes it a little easier for the home gardener to handle, the soil mix may be incompatible with that in your garden. Unfortunately, buying container trees may be the only way that you will be able to find the species or cultivar that you want. Just remember: the closer the soil content matches the type in your own garden, the less stress it will be for roots to become established. To try and overcome this problem, remove the plant carefully from the container and then "mutilate" the outer roots as one nursery puts it. Use your fingers, or a sharp trowel, if necessary, to tease them out so that they will make good contact with the soil in which they will grow.

When shopping for a tree in a container, try to judge how well it sits. Too loose means that you might be paying for as much soil as plant. Then, too, don't accept a tree that is obviously too small for its container with roots dangling out of the hole in the bottom. Even more important is to avoid a tree with kinked roots circling around the trunk at the soil line. It is a defect that can ultimately cause the death of the tree.

I've been quite satisfied with mail order tube plants from an Oregon nursery. Many of their trees are available in 6" deep disposable containers. The plants vary in size between 6" to 2' and are inexpensive to ship. I've planted them in a small nursery area for a year or two where their needs were easily met. When finally placed in their permanent locations, they were well on their way to becoming nice sized specimens.

Purchasing large container or balled-and-burlapped (B&B) trees through the mail is not usually an option because transportation costs can be prohibitive, so if you've decided on a good sized specimen, seek out a nursery or garden center as close to your home as possible.

In our heavy soils, especially when dealing with a hefty tree, I've had the most success when planting B&B stock. Before you buy such a tree from a nursery, look to see if it has an adequate earth ball for its height. A good rule of thumb is that a 1' tall tree should have a root ball at least 8" in size. Add 2" to the ball for every additional foot in height. Too small means that too many roots were cut when it was dug. Also, be wary of the plastic burlap that some nurseries use, and remove it completely. It will, of course, never disintegrate. Cloth burlap should be untied and placed as far under the plant as possible. In time, it will rot. One of the trees that I planted recently had a burlapped root ball enforced with heavy wire which the nurseryman insisted could be left it place. I planted it this way but think that this was a mistake because the roots appeared to be struggling to grow through it. Unlike planting containerized stock, handle B&Bs carefully so as not to break up any part of the earth ball. If the soil within it is very loose, it may have been added as the ball was being burlapped.

Before the scheduled delivery of your new tree, inquire as to the vehicle the nursery will use for transport. This is not just being nosy but important information that you should know, especially in dealing with small businesses. An open pick-up truck, unless it is covered completely with heavy tarps, may result in wind damage to your plants. You, too, should not transport any plant in such a vehicle.

Much has been written recently about the transplanting process itself. Yes, it is still true that digging a hole much larger than the root ball is advisable, but don't make it deeper than the ball itself. Enlarge the width of the hole rather than the depth. If drainage is not perfect, plant the tree slightly above grade. Back filling with amended soil is now considered by some to be a waste of good materials, but if not overdone, I don't think it can hurt, and may possibly help. To fill around the plant, mix at least a half of the original soil with compost or moistened peat moss.

Moving plants to a new environment is bound to be stressful for plants, and this is not the time to provide a big feed. Rather, withhold fertilizer for the time being. The second year after planting is time enough to supplement the nutrients already in the soil. How well I remember cringing as I watched a farmer place fresh manure in the hole of a tree that he was planting. He was treating it like one of his annual crops. But a tree is not an annual. For you, it may be everlasting. It's not a good idea to amend the soil early on with other than well-decomposed materials. After the tree is in place, apply a mulch about 2" deep, being careful not to come too close to the trunk which might create a constantly wet, disease- prone environment.

If the deciduous tree appears to be loose in its new home, it may require some staking. Also, don't forget its need for supplemental water in dry weather. Check this in autumn after leaf drop to be certain that as it enters its dormant stage, the root ball will have enough moisture to see it through the winter.

As the tree grows, sometimes suckers and sprouts come up from the base in early spring. Many species suffer from this problem which mars their appearance. At our place, native gray birch and some crabapples have this habit. Prune these interlopers away, by all means, or early in the season, use one of the products on the market that suppress new sucker growth for up to three months.

When should you plant that new tree? Hopefully, you will be able to do so immediately after delivery. Let us say that you plan garden time when you will be at home from work, but you're called out unexpectedly. Or when the tree arrives, so does a non-stop rain. Or you've sharpened your favorite spade, but it breaks off at the handle. If you receive the tree bare root, it can temporarily be heeled in the compost heap. Or if it is in a small tube, you can transfer it to a larger pot. You can hold on to a B&B or container plant for quite a few weeks providing that its root system is kept well watered. On at least one occasion, I've had to set aside B&B plants for a month or two storing them, meanwhile, in a place that was easy to water. Optimally, we should all try to plant hardwood trees in early spring or late fall planting. A few species, such as birch, beech, most oaks, dogwood, and magnolia, seem to do better if moved only in early spring.

Exceptional Flowering Trees:

There is scarcely an outdoor setting that has too many flowering trees. Like me, you may admire many, but your choice is certainly limited by your own particular design, space, and cultural necessities. This is true at our garden where I am somewhat restricted by our heavy, damp soils. Yet, quite a few of my recommendations are the glory of our garden in spring and summer. Then, too, many of these trees also provide additional interest with colorful fruit or seed pods and magnificent autumn foliage color. I describe my favorites below in order of their bloom time in the northern Mid-Atlantic states:

Late April:

Just as the foliage is returning to the deciduous trees, our star magnolia *(Magnolia stellata)* opens its creamy white flowers. We have it planted in a rock bed north of the house, a protected situation where the blooms are not hit by a late frost as is often the case. This magnolia has been growing slowly, but now, after many years, has reached 10' wide in width and 15' in height. Given more room, it would probably grow wider! Perhaps when you read this, a new hybrid stellata will be introduced with deep pink flowers.

The native shadblows *(Amelanchier canadensis)* are early blooming plants that I have seen growing in nearby woodland. They are perfect for a naturalistic garden. Their delicate, pretty white racemes are displayed on a shrub-like tree. If desired, this shrubby tree can be trained to one trunk.

I've planted the Higan cherry (*Prunus subhirtella* 'Autumnalis') for landscape clients who were always surprised that it flowers in both spring and autumn—not as profusely, though, in its secondary bloom. Give it plenty of room; it can grow 40' high and 30' wide.

Early May:

Our flowering dogwoods, both the hybrid *Cornus florida* 'Cherokee Princess' and our several self-sown seedling trees, begin to flower just as the other native trees come into leaf.

An unusually cool spring this year slowed them down a bit. Troubled in the past by several problems, East Coast dogwoods are now making quite a nice come-back, and thus, bringing us flocks of songbirds that devour the fruit. I've never met a healthy dogwood that I didn't like.

The silverbell, *Halesia tetraptera*, is a species that grows 25' tall and wide, with pretty, dainty white bells. I imagine that pink cultivars, such as 'Carolina', are even lovelier.

Crabapples are my special favorites because their blooms turn into attractive fruit at the end of the growing season. *Malus baccata*, the Siberian crab, is one of the earliest to bloom followed by *Malus floribunda*, a dependable old Japanese species, both moderately tall and broad.

Mid-May:

The warming of spring days brings a great many other flowering crabs into bloom, and new cultivars are always being introduced. In this older garden, I really cherish *Malus* 'Red Jade' a crab that has been available for a long time. It grows to only about 15', but its long, weeping branches are picture-perfect on a slight incline. Late in the growing season, 'Red Jade' sports bright red fruits, a stunning sight—before the birds find them. Equally as lovely is *Malus sargentii* with tiny red fruit in autumn. In height, this tree is probably the lowest of the crabs, but that doesn't mean it's small. Our twenty-seven year old specimen is 10' high, and must be 15' wide!

The Eastern redbud, *Cercis canadensis*, is a tree that I expect to plant in the near future. It is difficult to position near other plants because the blooms are an odd shade of purplish-pink. It does make a nice contrast with white flowering dogwoods. The purple leafed C. 'Forest Pansy' is a fine cultivar.

The red horsechestnut, *Aesculus x carnea*, is a large, round-shaped tree with rose-red candles. In some areas, disease mars the midsummer foliage. If so, look to cultivars such as A.c. 'Briotii' which are said to be immune. Better still, consult with your agricultural agent to find out the names of the best cultivars for your own area.

Late May, Early June:

The Japanese snowbell, *Styrax japonicum,* is a small tree which grows to about 20' in height and width. Like the silverbell, the little white flowers of these two trees look best when they dangle from a hill above you. 'Pink Chimes' is an utterly descriptive name of a snowbell cultivar.

The American yellowwood, *Cladrastis kentukea*, has white, wisteria-like blooms that are every bit as attractive as that ornamental vine. In its death throes here, it sported a few blooms, but die it did. I could not keep the tree alive in our poorly drained soils. You might do better even if you are in a cold location as hardiness is said not to be a problem.

The tree lilac, *Syringa reticulata,* is a clean-looking, upright, 30' species. Our cultivar here, *Syringa* 'Ivory Silk,' has long white racemes that are fragrant, and late blooming. Also, the foliage is quite free of mildew, a plus for any lilac.

Mid-June:

The Korean dogwood, *Cornus kousa,* is the longest blooming tree in our garden. It starts in late May and sometimes continues to display its white bracts well into July, although they gradually turn rosy. Later in the season, strawberry-like fruits ornament the tree. Unfortunately, most of our songbirds cannot eat them because of their large size. In the Orient, they are devoured by several primates, so gardeners here must contend with raking away the fallen fruits which can be a bit messy.

Early July:

Another Japanese tree, *Stewartia pseudocamellia,* is utterly dependable each year for its white 2" camellia-like flowers, quite a treat in our northern realm. It blooms for a very long time but rarely exhibits all of its flowers at once. Some gardeners may not like this trait. I particularly enjoy its exfoliating bark which stands out so nicely in the snow.

Late July, Early August:

The Korean bee tree, *Evodia daniellii,* is a tree I've only seen in botanical gardens, but if you don't have a shrub with white flowers late in the season, then this 30' tree might be just the ticket. The blooms eventually become dark red fruits followed by interesting seed capsules.

The Franklin tree (named after old Ben) *Franklinia alatamaha,* needs very well drained soils to thrive. If you have the right place and can locate a transplantable specimen, you'll have a treasure. It will then grow to 30' in height and display its five petaled white blossoms every year after it's established.

The sourwood, *Oxydendrum arboreum,* is a native tree with a pyramidal shape and blooms that resemble pieris. Mine is planted in too much shade, and thus, it only blooms at the top. However, I've seen this medium sized tree in groves along the Blue Ridge Parkway where it contributes wonderful late-season flower power.

The Japanese pagoda tree, *Sophora japonica,* is a large, round shaped tree that took forever to begin flowering for me. It did so at our first house only after many long years—just as we were about to move! Plant it if you think you'll be around for awhile to enjoy its lovely pale yellow panicles, and give the tree plenty of space.

It should be noted that time of bloom can differ slightly from one season to the next. An extraordinary four day hot spell, such as the one we experienced one April week, accelerated the flowering time of many of our plants, from perennials to trees. Then, too, height and width can also differ from one climatic area to another.

The above are not the only magnificent ornamental trees for the greater part of the U.S. but they are major species that are well worth a place in every garden where a suitable location can be found. Many other deciduous trees are grown not for the flower-fruit cycle but primarily for their pleasing shapes, summer foliage, or fall color. Favorites of mine in this category include the many Japanese maples; birch species that are white barked and free of insect damage; and the refined katsura, *Cercidiphyllum japonicum*, a large tree with graceful, wide-spreading branches and a rounded silhouette. A gardener can afford to be discriminating; the choice of a new tree is so delicious that when an old tree must come down, there is no need to fret. A lovely replacement is somewhere in the wings. Maybe the owner of a new home with a tree empty lot should not be pitied after all because he can be so selective about his new plantings! It is the flowering tree, above all else at Frog Pond Farm, that wins my heart, and I will always give it, as the English say, "pride of place."

When two years have gone by from the time you planted your new tree, there is one more important thing for you to do: stand back to observe and admire the results of your labor! If the tree has survived its first few years in good shape, chances are that it will continue to thrive. This is the time to pat yourself on the back for taking on a worthwhile task. In the final reckoning of your life's accomplishments, high on the list will be the fact that you have planted a beautiful tree.

CHAPTER XIV
HILLS, BANKS AND SLIPPERY SLOPES

CHAPTER XIV
Hills, Banks, and Slippery Slopes

Let's be level headed about deciding what to do if your property has any difficult-to-manage hills, banks, and slippery slopes. The slopes need not be severe in order to be awkward. Once, I almost lost my head—no, my feet!—at a garden wedding party that I was attending as a guest. Legs of the small tables set into the slightly sloping hillside lawn were not quite secure, and sitting on one of those pull-up chairs was an unsettling experience. Several times, I landed on my back, dinner plate and all.

Many a garden has such a lawn, and although the grade may not be steep enough to cause problems while mowing grass, it is less than an ideal spot for some outdoor activities. Dining alfresco demands a level area. Setting chairs on a slippery slope is an accident that is bound to happen.

This is not to say that every square foot of a garden must be strictly functional. In fact, a garden on a good-sized hilly property has a great many creative possibilities that are well worth exploring. On a pancake-flat piece of land, many designers go to great lengths to create changes of elevation. Why? Because the ups and downs of an undulating property are so appealing to the eye.

Try to imagine the scenery as you are driving on a mountain road. Every turn of the corner, every valley, every hill, reveals a new and exciting scene. On the other hand, imagine a long drive across the center of Florida. The road, without dip or rise, is surrounded by a sea of saw grass. Although the biologically trained mind may fully appreciate this seemingly unchanging flora, many drivers find it monotonous and struggle to stay awake.

In renovating your property, don't be in a hurry to create a level plain anywhere and everywhere. Variability is what creates interest. However, if you have places that were once gentle slopes but erosion has decreased their plant holding capacity, you've probably noticed how quickly weeds take over. You might be maintaining the slopes with a string trimmer, but this is a perpetual maintenance grind that you could well do without.

Here are some rules of thumb to help you evaluate the extent of your slopes: A slight hill might be defined as one with 10 percent of slope. Or, to put it another way, a slope of about 1' in rise to a 10' length is described as a 1 to 10 slope. This could probably be well maintained in lawn grass if not leveled for a patio. A moderate hill has 20 percent of slope or a rise of 2' to a 10' length. Although some homeowners plant such sites in lawn, they will be far easier to maintain with one or more groundcovers. A steep slope is a bank with 30 percent of slope or 3' in rise to a 10' length. I have seen such slopes planted with grass in many public gardens, and well remember one in an old Irish estate garden called Powerscourt. The chief groundskeeper told us that they were maintained by special mowing machines without wheels that float on a cushion of air, and that by means of ropes, the machines must be pulled up to the top of the slope when they have completed a cycle. While such extraordinary treatment may be possible in gardens with large budgets and ample labor, most of us would probably be far better off terracing such steep banks.

The hilly parts of your garden that might need work could be described as one or more of the following:

Your slightly sloping lawn of grasses never gets a clean, even mowing.

Moderately sloping banks are losing lawn grasses to weeds.

With every rainfall, your downhill sloping banks are sending more and more soil into your driveway, your neighbor's property, or maybe even out onto your roadway.

Planted hillsides on a windy north or northwest exposure often have foliage that has become tattered and torn.

Planted hillsides in full sun have become difficult to irrigate during a drought and are severely parched by midsummer.

Wet, muddy banks are now covered with unwanted vegetation rather than ornamental plants.

Old, overgrown trees on some slopes shade out all other low vegetation.

Steep slopes are never able to hold new plants despite your noblest efforts to get them established.

If your slight hillside is covered with lawn grasses, mowing should not be difficult. Yet, there are some conditions under which these places always look unkempt and uneven. It may be that the cutting blades of your mower need to be sharpened more often. Or, perhaps, the lawn was originally planted with too fine a grass seed for a satisfactory cut in this area. High traffic areas sometimes suffer this problem. If this bothers you, you'll probably get the result that you want by replanting with a sturdier, coarser type of lawn grass.

In dealing with any problem slope where you've decided to start from scratch and plant a groundcover other than grass, consider the following:

Drainage:

If any of your slopes have become eroded through the passing of many years, the first line of attack is to correct all drainage problems. Where they are truly severe, you may have to call in a landscape engineer with experience in these matters. A halfhearted attempt on your part to eliminate water damage could result in ruining other parts of your property, or, even worse, it might send flood waters down to your neighbor. Don't underestimate the value of good drainage. It's crucial to the success of every garden.

Seasonal considerations:

The best possible time to rejuvenate a slope with a new groundcover is in spring which will give new plants plenty of time to become established before cold weather arrives. On the other hand, if, you are overly hasty to get the job done too early in the season, you might actually make the matter worse, especially on heavy clay soils. When you work wet, spongy ground too early in the season, soil compaction is bound to occur. This might be a great source of material for pottery but few plants can withstand this treatment. Although compacted clay soil makes it impossible to grow fine plants, weeds don't seem to mind at all.

Improper tools:

Don't attempt to treat any slope as though it were a vegetable garden by working it with a rototiller. This is not the place to use a tiller. Your objective here should be to stabilize the soil not soften it.

Fill:

Hold off with filling and leveling empty holes and pockets where old plants have been removed. To do this too far ahead of the planting date may cause more soil to float downhill after a heavy rainstorm. When you are ready to fill deep gouges where plants have been removed, it's just as well to use inexpensive fill dirt and save better topsoil or compost for establishing your new groundcover plants.

Weed Preventatives:

On all banks, avoid using herbicides which might possibly wash downward and land in concentrated pockets around some plants susceptible to injury

Other Considerations:

Where there is some erosion on moderate to steep slopes, existing groundcovers are forever in a competing battle. Replanting them with more suitable species might improve the situation. One of the shrubs that we successfully used early in our landscaping efforts here at Frog Pond Farm was the cutleaf stephandra *(Stephanandra incisa)*. Planted soon after house construction on newly graded slopes, our bank of stephandra quickly took hold with its considerable root-running capacities. These are shrubs that reach 5' in height or more; even better, I think, is the new cultivar *Stephanandra incisa* 'Crispa', which is lower in height. Either is guaranteed to fully cover both moderate and fairly steep slopes and save you the time and exertion of perpetual weeding. Stephandra, however, does look like a maze of twiggy branches in the winter so is best used away from window views.

Whatever groundcover you plant, you will first have to eliminate any weeds during the first few years to shorten the establishment period. Start, at least, with a clean slate.

In dealing with shrubs, "dishing" the new plant, or holding the soil around it with slightly embedded rocks on the lower side, is very helpful. The rocks can be left in place until the plants are well established, or they can later be covered with a mulch.

On our waterlogged banks which were originally level and planted to grass (such as the edges of our pond), we eventually planted several root-binding clumps of the yellow flag iris *(Iris pseudacorus)*, the Japanese iris *(Iris ensata)*, and the Siberian iris *(Iris sibirica)*. All thrive in such places. Not only are they lovely in bloom, but water-side iris are also perfect hiding places for frogs!

If you have a similar situation, and if shrubs of a moderate height are not objectionable, then you might try native red osier dogwoods *(Cornus sericea)* which are particularly attractive because of their flaming red twigs in winter, or the equally dramatic yellow-stemmed C.s. 'Flaviramea'. You'll have to space these shrubs wide apart as they can grow quite large, but in a short time, they will grow together. Early each spring, cut them quite low to the ground to encourage colorful new growth.

This spring, I've been hoping to plant the west bank of our pond with the low, dense foliaged willow *Salix purpurea* where it will grow to 2' tall. Another willow that I tried, *Salix repens* variety *nitida*, was unsuccessful in this position because its slim branches were a little too slow-growing for covering the bank. Contrary to common belief, not all willows are take-over plants.

Where a great many deciduous trees block all vestiges of sunlight on your slope or bank, even your most stalwart shade loving ornamentals beneath them might fail. In this case, either cut down some of the trees and/or limb them up considerably so that more light will penetrate the canopy. If neither answer pleases you, but yet you want flowers, concentrate on ephemerals…those plants that bloom early in the season before shade is a problem. Early bulbs, such as species tulips, narcissus, crocuses, snowdrops, etc., will bloom under such conditions.

Riprapping:

Plants cannot solve every problem situation. One of them is what to do with the muddy verges along a stream or pond where you would like to move close to the water. Geese and other water fowl don't seem to mind this condition but you do! It can be frustrating when you want to stand at the water's edge without ruining your shoes. The answer might be riprapping—assembling rocks in a thick layer over such a bank. Broken stones can also be used for this purpose. If you intend to walk on them, make sure the rocks are not sharp.

Recommended Groundcover Plants:

As you await the arrival of proper conditions for slope renovation, you can busy your-self by purchasing the plants that you will need. Looking through several references, you'll find list upon list of lovely little low plants, such as *Paxistima canbyi*, the false boxwood. It may be perfect for small gardens, but if you want to cover a good sized area quickly, you'll need sturdier stuff with root running capacities. Try to select species that grows as quickly as possible to shorten the weeding period as much as possible.

I'll tell you what I've discovered about some of the best groundcovers that I have grown myself or installed for others. Just a few that come to mind, excellent for sunny banks, include some of the lower cotoneasters, especially the rockspray or herringbone cotoneas-ter, *C. horizontalis*. Its interesting branches look wonderful when splayed across a slope. Unfortunately, this rockspray, like the cranberry cotoneaster, *C. apiculatus*, or the 18" tall creeping cotoneaster, *C. adpressus*, is deciduous in the winter. If this is not a problem, they are among the very best of low groundcovers.

Another good choice is the semi-evergreen willow-leafed, *Cotoneaster salicifolius* 'Scarlet Leader', growing only a foot tall and noted for its brilliant red autumn fruit. Not all coto-neasters have abundant berries, however. The bearberry cultivar, *C.dammeri* 'Skogholm', grows fast and wide, but its fruits are disappointedly sparse. C.d. 'Coral Beauty' appears to be much better in this regard but is otherwise similar. Don't take catalogues too literally when they describe the autumn display. It is far better to visit a nursery in autumn and judge for yourself.

Combining two or more species of shrubs on one slope might be a good idea for con-trast of leaf form. Whatever living carpets you select, keep each group massed rather than interspersed or you'll eventually have a rat's nest on your hands.

Many gardeners plant entire slopes with junipers, particularly low types like *Juniperus horizontalis*, *J. squamata*, or *J. sabina*. In an area to be heavily planted, too much of one thing can be rather a bore, so resist that nursery's offer of a special deal on a large quantity of junipers. If you do use junipers, select prostrate forms such as J.h. 'Prostrata' that really flatten themselves against the soil. If you wish, they can be combined in groupings with slightly more upright shrubs to break up the expanse. In one of my myrtle areas, I created a little more interest by opening up a broad section with heavily rooted hostas. The effect is quite pleasing, at least, in summer.

A low conifer that I have grown in a sun-baked spot (after providing a sandy niche) is the shore juniper, *Juniperus conferta*, with needles that have a texture all their own, like soft, tiny brushes. It's best, I think, for cascading over a brick, rock or tie wall. In such a position, I find it much more appealing than many other junipers.

If your sloping hillside is in the dappled shade of existing trees, you may want to use one of the three most common groundcovers, hardy ivy, pachysandra, or myrtle *(Vinca minor)*. There is always a reason why some things are more popular than others. When it comes to shady area groundcovers, the big three have proven themselves to be reliable grass substitutes. However, in many Pacific Northwestern gardens, ivy has now become a noxious pest, and in some East Coast areas, myrtle, too, has become invasive, so do check their status in your area before you commit yourself to a planting that could run out of control.

Where it is hardy, another fine shade lover (out of the prevailing wind) is the dwarf Oregon grape holly, *Mahonia repens*. Because these plants are expensive to use en masse, it is best to consider them only for small areas. This mahonia is a true root runner; it grows at a rather slow but steady place. Thus, you will have to plant them close together to have cover within a reasonable period of time.

One of the most difficult slopes to plant is a shady, windy hillside facing north or northwest. A plant that I count on for such an exposure, in this, a Mid-Atlantic state, is the drooping leucothoe, *L. fontanesiana*, sometimes called the fetter bush. Be warned, though, if you are troubled with deer visitations. Leucothoe is one of their favorite food plants. If deer are not a problem, and if the soil is reasonably moist, you will rarely go wrong with this species. It does require a bit of pruning to remove a few dead branches after an exceptionally cold winter.

If a little more shade would be desirable on your uphill bank, you might plant small, specimen trees such as the Carolina silverbell, *Halesia monticola*, or the Japanese snowbell, *Styrax japonicum*. Both ring as true to their names with bell-like blossoms that are best seen looking up and into them. Hanging below the styrax branches in late summer and early fall are lovely greenish white fruits suspended below the branches like tiny grapes.

Dry, sunny hillsides are a totally different proposition. The low bearberry, *Arctostaphylos uva-ursi*, is often recommended for such situations particularly where the soil is a sandy loam. Forget about this plant if your soils are heavy clay as here at Frog Pond Farm. Where happy, bearberry is extremely useful and as prostrate as they come, rooting all up and down its joints,. Many new cultivars are now in the marketplace, one with exceptionally large red fruits in autumn and another with red stems.

In full sun, you might plant the Scotch broom, *Cytisus decumbens*. It's nice for using over a retaining wall where its pea-like foliage and yellow flowers look their best. There are taller forms of this species also.

In addition, where hardy, you can carpet a sunny hillside with ground hugging sedums, or perhaps with ice plants *(Delospermas)*. Both are succulent plants that are often grown as perennials. Purchasing the great many needed for a groundcover might be quite expensive. If you find this to be the case, both species usually germinate readily from seed, or if you have stock plants, from cuttings. Delosperma has rather recently been introduced from South Africa, so not all species will winter well in cold areas. A friend recommended *Delosperma brunsthaleri* as one species that seems to be especially hardy. Where suitably perennial, it is surely a possibility for covering sunny, gritty slopes. Before you go whole hog, try a few.

I've seen an entire sunny slope planted with the 4" tall *Sedum spurium* 'Dragon's Blood' at the Ohme Rock Garden in the state of Washington. It is a variety generally hardy through Zone 4. Ohme's planting must be a dramatic sight in midsummer when covered with red flowers. If it does well for you, the effect will be a lovely mass of color and form.

On a bank where it is difficult to replace or amend the poor soil, there are several taller perennials that do well. One of my favorites for this situation is the obedient plant, *Physostegia virginiana*. A variegated form of it is a real show piece. However, if you plant the species, be prepared to really like it because you'll soon have a great many more than you expect.

Despite your attempts to replant a slope with ground-holding species, the area may simply be too steep to achieve satisfactory results. A retaining wall or two is then probably necessary. If you already have walls that need some work, or you feel ambitious enough to rework your slope with a new wall, then read on to Chapter XV.

CHAPTER XV
UP THE WALL

CHAPTER XV
Up The Wall

If you live on a hilly property, are all those steep embankments in your garden driving you "up the wall?" Some of them might have been terraced with retainers, but if age has taken its toll, the walls could need repair or replacement. Or, if all your slopes are covered with groundcovers, you might now want to create more interest by adding a new wall or two. As retainers slice into a hillside, both horizontal terraces and dramatic drops are created. When adequately constructed and appropriately planted, they can become one of the most sensational features in your garden.

Retaining walls can be built of railroad ties, pressure treated timbers, concrete pavers, concrete blocks, bricks, dry-laid or mortared stone. One of the greatest advantages of using recycled railroad ties is that they make good use of lumber that has already been harvested, thus sparing some of the trees in our forests. There are also unorthodox materials that you might use. If, by any chance, your landscape renovation includes breaking up slabs of an old concrete patio, or if you know of a place where concrete is being removed, then you might investigate the possibility of building retaining walls with this otherwise unattractive material. In the country of New Zealand, we were impressed by slabs of discarded concrete used by several of its innovative gardeners as handsome slope retainers or free standing garden divisions.

Constructing retaining walls furnished with rock plants is one way of creating a splendid feature. Walls such as these allow you to grow billowing mounds on their terraces with spill-overs that cascade down their sides. Sometimes, you can also add creepers that cling to the walls themselves. They are especially dramatic in spring and early summer, and particularly advantageous if the walls are built on an upward slope from your house or some other frequently used vantage point. Although they can be effective in lightly shaded areas, walls in full sun provide the greatest opportunity for an exuberant flower display.

The double-tiered dry-laid rock walls here at Frog Pond Farm, built of stone collected from our roadways, are on a downward slope from the house leading to the pond below our house. Because of this, I planted all-season broadleaf shrubs for low-maintenance in an area where rock plants cannot be seen from our house windows. A 3-4' deep strip below these walls is the site of tall perennials that are at their best in summer when we venture more frequently into this part of our garden.

Ever since Babylonian times, terraced retaining walls have been considered the ultimate in bank treatment. Wherever you look in British, French, or Italian gardens, you will find old walls perhaps 3' to 12' in height. Although some of these structures were specifically designed to protect tender plants from climatic extremes, low retainers on hillsides are also used in places where soil tends to wash away with every storm.

Tall walls, I think, look best in spacious surroundings. American gardeners on modest sized properties would be well advised to try and avoid those that rise without a break to a great height. Use, instead, two or three tiers rather than one. Against my advice, a client of mine (who happened to be a builder) went ahead and constructed a 12' high railroad tie wall without any setbacks. It enclosed a patio that could not have been more than 25' wide. Needless to say, it looked formidable which is a polite way of saying "terrible." Then, too, it took many years for the climbers I planted on the patio side and the cascading plants above the wall to soften this hard look.

Recently, I visited a plant collector's amazing acquisitions on a steep slope and was surprised that the two foot high edging was only a "farmer's collection" of rubble and rocks. So fascinating were the plants on the bank that I could only lament a lost opportunity. Here was an ideal place to build a garden with real rock walls to blend in with the existing environment. Using indigenous rock is a most satisfactory way of treating soils that are forever spitting up boulders from beneath the surface.

Even the most ambitious do-it-yourselfer should realize that constructing retaining walls over 3' in height requires equipment and techniques best entrusted to experienced professionals, and this can be an expensive proposition. Consider, though, that it is a waste of time and effort for you to attempt to create a wall with only small stones. The results are almost always miserly. But then, there are what I call "in-betweens"—large rocks that even a fairly strong woman can lift. Building low, dry-laid rock walls with these "in-betweens" is something for you to consider doing on your own, especially if you have a ready supply of rocks. Many homeowners can handle them if they exercise extreme care to avoid injury. What is also required is a large dose of patience to lay the rocks as level as possible.

Properly placed rocks set horizontally into a slope, each layer overlapping the other, do a very good job of securing a bank. The walls, themselves, should lean inward toward the bank to make them stronger. One of the advantages of using rocks, rather than timbers, is that the wall can be so easily curved during the construction period.

Level terraces between two walls can be a devil to weed and so, make them wide enough to accommodate both the plants and the weeder's feet because there will be times when you might need to climb up into them. In dealing with rock plants, a gravel mulch will help to impede unwanted vegetation.

Perhaps you might want to consider the ultimate treatment for a steep slope, one that is retained by several tiers of walls and includes a series of switchback paths with steps winding up to an overlook at the very top. A recirculated pool and waterfall can be a beautiful addition to this kind of a development. However, a project of this complexity requires far more information than I can offer you from my experience, so before you start, further study and planning will be necessary.

Here is another approach that might be the answer if you already have one high dry-laid stone wall terracing a slope rather than several terraces and drops. In this case, plant the crevices or pockets between the rocks. This can become the home to a great variety of alpine-like perennials with creeping or cascading habits. Whatever the height of your wall, it is essential that you tilt the rocks backward into the slope so that rainwater can reach the crevice plants.

It is far easier to fill crevices with plants as a wall is being constructed. However, if the wall is already in place, some of the rocks may have shifted and need to be realigned. There can be no better time to set in your new plants. Absent this opportunity, you can still fill some small crevices by first covering the root systems of strong seedlings or cuttings with clumps of damp clay, and then carefully wedging them into place.

A fine example of a crevice planted wall is the rock retainer at the Morris Arboretum at the University of Pennsylvania. What is so fascinating about it is that none of the delightful perennials planted in the rock pockets, at the time when I observed them, were particularly rare or unusual. This might be the way for you to go—unless you are a high alpine enthusiast. As with all landscaping projects, if you are starting from scratch in furnishing a renovated or newly constructed wall, it's a good idea to search out and examine similar structures and their plantings elsewhere before you even begin your work.

If you are dealing with any alpines, especially those denizens of high mountains, a gritty, stony type of soil is necessary to accommodate them. Almost all these plants require excellent drainage. Gardeners who enjoy high alpines can take advantage of the countless number of species that actually prefer sending their roots deep down through the kind of gravely mixture that is found on a mountainside.

A great deal of detailed information about building and planting rock retaining walls is available from the North American Rock Garden Society. Much of it is essential knowledge if wall building is entirely new to you. Unfortunately, in low-elevation areas, those of us in the Mid-Atlantic states who become involved with true alpines (the epitome of wall plantings) will probably find that summer heat, humidity, and an inconstant snow cover all too often result in poor plant longevity. Happily, there are quite a few species that are long lived and will adapt to lowland conditions (except in the deep South) and where well situated, are able to bloom with such abandon that it touches one's heart to realize that any living thing can be so lovely. Although highland gardeners have an enormous range of plant choices, lowland gardeners who prepare their soils carefully so that they are well drained, can usually grow many forms of arabis, aubretia, aurina, campanula, dianthus, true geraniums, helianthemum, iberis, ground pinks and creeping phlox, saponaria, mossy saxifrages, and thyme. The list is far more extensive, and then, too, within each genus there are sometimes species or cultivars that are particularly easy to grow. There are also some high altitude meadow species that adapt to low elevation plantings. Growing rock plants can become a fascinating hobby, particularly useful for those with small, hilly gardens who want to cultivate a large variety of plants.

If the view of your wall is in plain sight for most of the year, concentrate on selecting some plants that are evergreen. When you arrange such things, you will also want to give a great deal of consideration to achieving pleasing foliage and flower color combinations.

A raised bed with a rock retainer is another possibility when there is little or no ground slope. To grow some of these lovely plants, my husband and I built two such beds in our meadow garden. They are not too bad, although not nearly as natural looking as if we were working on a steep slope with rocky outcroppings. Nevertheless, these low retainers gave us a special place to fill with well drained soil. Throughout the years, these raised beds have undergone a variety of plantings with nature gradually eliminating the most diminutive of the alpines. In our own erratic climate, I've come to realize that two, three, four years of splendor are just about as long as I can expect from those plants that originated on the very highest parts of mountains. In their place, I've been concentrating more on the rock plants that I listed earlier To prepare for the future, when age will no longer allow me to fuss about with any plant that might be called "iffy," I've also begun to include several low, more permanent shrubs such as *Daphne x burkwoodii* 'Somerset' and *Spiraea bumalda* 'Crispa'.

If the retaining walls that you want to create or renovate are complex structures that require professional assistance, don't bother to call upon the fellow who only mows lawns for a living. As in many aspects of landscape renovation, leaving the construction of large walls entirely in the hands of the inexperienced is bound to be disappointing. Try to find a contractor who has already built satisfactory retainers. On the other hand, if you are trying to repair walls that are not too high or broad, and even the largest of your stones is not beyond your lifting ability, an inexperienced helper might be all you need to help with their rearrangement. By all means, set the plants in place yourself because it is this phase of the project that will require your feel for the artistic.

Then, too, seldom will one nursery or one garden center be able to supply you with exactly the species that you seek. Locating the right plant for the location that you have in mind may mean dealing with several sources, many of them mail order. So take your time, buy a minimum of three of a kind to create a mass, and if you must, choose smaller sized plants than you might prefer and give them time to develop. Don't fall for a substitute species that is not quite perfect for the task at hand. Having accomplished all this, it should not surprise you if that once difficult-to-maintain hillside turns out to be the pride of your entire garden.

CHAPTER XVI
OUR LAND OF PLENTY—PLENTY OF PESTS

Natalia Petrunyk

CHAPTER XVI
Our Land of Plenty—Plenty of Pests

"Attract Wildlife!" It's a proclamation echoed over and over again in our garden literature. Songbirds, presumably, head the list of creatures that enhance the garden scene, and a great many of us go to some effort to provide them with the food, shelter, and nesting materials that will draw them close to our line-of-sight.

At Frog Pond Farm, as one would expect, it is also the bullfrog who entertains us, and it is his deep-throated croak that we welcome each summer as a signal to us that all is right in our little world. Butterflies, too, are tempted to stay here, and so we plant many flowers that are good nectar food. And then there's the bat that has lived for years amid the rafters of our deck. It's amazing what a thorough job he does in ridding our place of pesky mosquitoes! The occasional red foxes and the wild turkeys that trot about now and then in our meadow are always viewed with excitement. Black bears are here, too, in the northern part of our state, but where they are not too numerous, these omnivorous animals seldom do serious harm to either people or their plantings.

But should we attract all wildlife? The older garden, which you've been renovating with a pleasing assortment of plants, is an especially attractive mecca for many critters. How much we enjoy the gray squirrels that delight us with their acrobatic antics! Yet, these little animals are not content to gather the woodland's nuts and seeds. Their first choice is to compete at the feeder for seed we've put out for the birds. Chipmunks, too, gather there to feed, one at a time, but under our pine trees, they sometimes dislodge my tiny, seed-grown tubers of cyclamen, a minor problem I've decided. And then there are occasional raccoons, those delightfully resourceful creatures, but they inevitably steal the suet and its container that we leave for the birds. Only an occasional rabbit, the Eastern cottontail, visits us--which is more than a good many gardeners can say—but I can truly sympathize with Beatrix Potter's Mr. MacGregor who banned Peter Rabbit from his vegetable patch. And in rural areas, woodchucks (also called groundhogs) can devastate many plantings, especially those in vegetable gardens.

Yet, all these creatures, or many others, depending upon where you live, were tenants of the land before we arrived. Regardless of the problems that they sometimes create, it is good to know that some wildlife is still with us. Mother Nature sometimes takes care of imbalance when it occurs, and unless you live in a densely populated area with a minimum of introduced flora, the chances are that some birds and animals will visit you without an invitation. You need not lift a finger to attract them.

There are, however, two pests whose populations have exploded into such great numbers that they threaten not only the stability of our forests but our health and the entire ecosystem in which we garden. Perhaps, in the future, a poster of these two will hang on the walls of your post office:

<u>Public Enemy Number 1,</u> <u>white tailed deer;</u> <u>Public Enemy Number 2,</u> <u>the Canada goose.</u>

Public Enemy No. 1:

Deer, of one sort or another, are present in every one of our 48 contiguous states, and they do incredible damage to farm and garden plants wherever they have over-multiplied. That means almost everywhere. If Bambi were as ugly as Godzilla, as clumsy as a baboon, or as slimy as a snake, then few people would become emotional about finding ways to reduce their numbers. Some animal lovers cherish this population explosion. A community near us has actually found it necessary to propose an ordinance banning its residents from feeding deer. Indeed, few of us can resist the charm of these beautiful animals, but should we encourage their great numbers? I think not when I remember how awful is the sight of a carcass along the roadside, the result of a car accident. It is also a sign that the driver might have been hurt.

Early in June one year, a two week old fawn squeezed between the wires of our wooden gate into the garden. After romping for awhile, the fawn discovered that she could not leave because of the high fencing. She began butting her head against this polypropylene shield. As I tried to push her out the front gate, the little creature let out the most horrendous shriek. My husband came running, lifted her up, and carried the fawn onto the road. Bambi, of course, is incredibly adorable with its spotted coat, big brown eyes, and perky ears. Yet, all serious gardeners should realize that a way must be found to decrease deer numbers.

There are, in fact, far more white tailed deer now in Eastern U.S.A. then in 1620 when the Pilgrims settled here. In our early history, predators, such as wolves and coyotes, helped to keep excessive populations in check, but a look at a century old cookbook tells more of the story. These books usually included recipes for venison steak, coon pie, roasted goose, and possum stew. Hunters, not supermarkets, supplied many a family's dining table with fresh meat. Overpopulation of animals was not a problem in those days because society remedied the situation very nicely. Hunting was encouraged as a means of providing sustenance for many a family. As recently as thirty–five years ago, when we first moved to the countryside, boys and girls in high school were excused from their studies during the autumn or early winter season so that they could participate in the hunt. These days, perhaps because our attitudes about killing have undergone a serious appraisal, hunting is not nearly as popular.

As every gardener today in deer country knows, these animals are horticultural connoisseurs. I've never seen them eating thistles, nor do they seem to favor the multiflora roses that we are trying to eliminate from our garden verges. Deer seem to have the most voracious appetite for the plants around our homes that are well weeded, watered and fertilized. As you, the renovating gardener, bestow tender, loving care on your new plant acquisitions as well as on older ornamentals that you are possibly revitalizing, white tailed deer will show their appreciation by gobbling them up as they have just reached the peak of their beauty. Adding insult to injury is that the reproductive system of does will be further improved by the consumption of well cultivated plants. Some females are able to have three fawns each season rather than one or two.

Many gardeners apply deterrent sprays, smelly soaps, netting, unwashed human hair placed amidst plant foliage, all manner of things to discourage the deer, but these methods are of short-term value. Eventually, even if you plant a species recommended as "deer proof", Bambi and family might foil your plans, tasting some plants that might even be toxic to their systems. Without protective fencing around your cultivated areas, these four legged gourmets will treat your garden as though it were a four star restaurant.. munch, munch, munch.

High fencing, solidly secured, will protect your garden from marauding deer. One July afternoon, when our newly installed polypropylene fence was being tested, we discovered a breach. A doe had slipped through a section where the ground clips had come loose. Before my husband was able to locate the problem, the doe ate a belly-full of azaleas just beginning to form buds for next year, and then proceeded to dine on my few shrub roses. Next, she shredded the foliage of some of our hostas concentrating on the finest of our specimens. Every tall summer phlox, carefully selected by me because they are mildew resistant, as well as several other perennials, were also nipped in the bud. Then she turned to my potted plants on the patio and quickly devoured every lovely blue flower on a special container form of my morning glories. As a final dinner touch, she nibbled on the leaves of our weeping Red Jade crab apple, and then sifted through the bird seed in our rear feeder. Before she could decide on a dessert, my husband plugged the gap in the fence through which she had entered and shooed her out of our garden. Given enough time, the gardener in deer country will find that these animals will renovate your garden for you, but not for the better.

If I have scarcely mentioned deer damage before in the other chapters, it is because I believe that even one of these animals, but especially roving herds of many, are completely incompatible with landscape gardening. Although this may sound self-evident, all too many gardeners hope for the best and begin their garden renovation without first addressing this problem. If you live where deer have over-populated, sooner or later you will relax your vigil, forget to apply repellents and/or other deterrent gadgets, or you will plant something new and exciting forgetting that the deer might also find it new and exciting.

There are really only two ways of keeping deer off your property. Impenetrable fencing is necessary wherever possible. The other is to significantly reduce deer numbers in your area by severely culling the population. For some time in the future, both will probably be a necessary part of protecting our landscape plantings.

It is all well and good to realize that the use of firearms is never to be taken lightly. Besides, when it comes to deer, who can deny that they are splendid creatures, a true manifestation of "nature the beautiful" one might say? At our property it gives us ambiguous pleasure to observe the deer at a distance quietly going about their business of eating. However, a study by University of Pennsylvania says that where deer populations exceed 15 per sq. mile, the environment is affected adversely. In one area of our county, a helicopter survey counted 148.75 deer per square mile! Statisticians find it difficult to keep up with the growing numbers, but farmers in deer country, without protective crop fencing, know that they might cause millions of dollars worth of losses each year. One thing is for sure: too many deer in one area are a plague upon the land, and it is time to admit that something should be done to control these ever-growing herds.

A night drive through suburbs or countryside, and even on major highways, can have many an anxious moment as deer unexpectedly dart across a road. During the day, also, they can appear out of seemingly nowhere although deer are more active at dusk and dawn. Life in deer country means that automobile drivers must be constantly vigilant to avoid collisions. Damage to each car frequently amounts to several thousand dollars, and even worse, deer accidents sometimes result in the deaths of the driver and/or their passengers.

But of all the problems excessive deer populations create, perhaps the one with the most long-ranged consequences is the destruction of biodiversity. This is the term that ecologists use to describe a healthy relationship between the environment and its many living organisms. When it comes to natural areas, the decrease of biodiversity everywhere on the globe has become an important issue, and here it is on our very doorstep. In our area, deer are ravishing many sapling trees, such as oak, hickory, ash, and Canadian hemlock, and destroying the balance of nature in many other ways as well. Deer are also exceedingly fond of acorns, but if their numbers are too large, they may eventually displace the squirrels and chipmunks that also need their share. Deer can do a job on native groundcovers, and, it seems, particularly enjoy the taste of wild lilies, trilliums, orchids, and other beloved wildflowers. It can get complicated because, as a local naturalist points out, when a particular plant, such the native lupine, is eliminated by deer, a chain of events is set in motion. In the case of the lupine, it will mean the end of an endangered butterfly that relies on lupines for its food. Biologists can give us many other examples of biodiversity being limited by deer overpopulations.

It is the goal of many conservation organizations to preserve plants, animals, clean water, and natural communities by purchasing large tracts of land before housing developers destroy those pristine environments. These are worthwhile objectives, but where unaddressed overpopulations of any animal are involved, true land preservation may well be impossible.

Transporting excessive numbers of deer to other locations has been tried, but the animals are essentially of such nervous temperaments that they usually do not survive such a move. Immuno-contraception (birth control for female deer) may eventually prove successful when and if its many thorny problems can be solved. But can we wait any longer while our environment is being destroyed?

Meanwhile, back in the garden, many homeowners struggle to maintain their own private haven. When renovating your garden in deer country, the installation of fencing should take precedence over all other improvements.

There are many types of fencing that exclude deer. Some gardeners have had great success with electric fencing, but we have found it to be ineffective except for short-term use. Farmers in our area favor the wired fence 8' tall, and others prefer two parallel fences 5' apart and 5' in height. My husband installed a 7 ½' high polypropylene mesh fence strung from tree to tree and also from wooden posts 15' apart. He used the heaviest weight poly that he could purchase and secured it firmly at soil level. For us, one of the most pleasant things about this kind of fencing is that it is completely transparent and, in fact, can scarcely be seen unless close-up. The height, 7 ½', has worked out well because, if an occasional deer should find a gap and enter the garden, the stressed out animal would be able to escape up and over. This is all to the good if the homeowner is not home and able to open his gates.

Public Enemy No. 2:

They look like the Canada goose and act like the Canada goose, but most of those that we see year-round in our parks, fields, and gardens have never been to Canada. In all probability, their parents, grandparents, and great grandparents have never been there either. The Canada goose is a superlatively interesting bird, but my concern is with the non-migrating kind that has lost its instinct to make seasonal migrations. Its habits are deceptive because these geese honk in flight and frequently fly locally in V formations like their migrating cousins. Having multiplied in enormous numbers, they are almost as vexing as deer throughout many parts of our country. Quite a few cities and towns have been trying to solve what has become their ever-expanding populations. These strong, beautiful, intelligent birds are smart enough to take advantage of man's generosity in providing them with such lovely all-year grazing grounds that they no longer need to fly south in the winter. Seattle, Washington, is but one of many places where beaches and lakes must be frequently closed to bathers because of filthy goose droppings. In some places, it has also become a serious health hazard concerning drinking water. Each mature goose defecates from one to three pounds every day, and all too often, that is in the path of man.

In many states, the goose population is so bad that border collie patrols are being used to frighten the birds by herding them and chasing them off lakes, ponds, and lawns. It is a never ending chore, and even if the dogs temporarily frighten off the geese, these birds may return another year in full force after nesting on neighborhood properties

At our country home, Canadas would quickly pollute the spring water in our pond and brooks, our grassy areas, and our plantings-- if we permitted them to do so. A good deal of time must be spent every April disturbing these winged visitors when they land on the water so that they will not be able to begin their nest building routine. But occasionally, we are not successful, and we must tolerate the geese for a long while. Always in our minds is the realization that one nesting pair equals six to eight large Canadas by mid-summer, all of whom might very well return to build their own nests in future years.

Every year that passes by, goose increases go far beyond the carrying capacity of many suburbs and much of our countryside. One solution that might work is to destroy the eggs laid by every nesting non-migrating Canada. Eventually, there should be a significant population decline.

Activists for animal rights argue about every proposed new ordinance to limit excessive animal numbers. I look at it this way: Law enforcement agencies seek to locate criminals who burglarize, and no person is allowed to desecrate a property without being prosecuted. Yet, those who profess an unconditional love for deer and non-migrating Canadas feel that animals that desecrate and burglarize are beyond disapproval, beyond the law, beyond man's ability to correct situations that imperil our health, our safety, and our artistic endeavors. We have waited too long to address these problems, but then again, it is never too late.

Meanwhile, if the so-called Canada goose and/or white tailed deer have overpopulated your area, you should support community action to cull excessive numbers of these intolerable pests. Attracting wildlife to your garden has its limits.

CHAPTER XVII
WHERE TO FIND INSPIRATION

CHAPTER XVII.
Where To Find Inspiration

It's a hot, sunny summer day. You sit in the shade of your patio attached to your chair like moss affixed to a rock. What better time, you think, to decide which area of your garden is most in need of landscape renovation. Difficult as it is to desert the comforts of the shade, you walk around a bit to examine those places that have really been bothering you. Last week, when the weather was more invigorating, you had determined to remove some of your overgrown conifers. This week, you decide that they really are not so bad and do not need to be replaced. And then there's that steep, grass eroded slope that is so difficult to mow. In the heat of this day, improving it doesn't seem imperative. A better idea is to immediately sign up for a trip to Alaska which is sure to be pleasantly cool.

Procrastination, that thief of time, is part of being human, and we all suffer from it at one time or another. But sooner or later, the dedicated gardener will not be able to escape the fact that anticipated projects should now be in the planning stage. Since it is inspiration that fuels activity, maybe that is what you need to get you started. But human beings are a capricious lot, and the kind of inspiration that worked for you in the past might no longer motivate you today.

An old Chinese proverb says: "a single conversation with a wise man is worth a month's study of books." How true this was for me when I was twenty-five years old and wondering what on earth I should do with the barren lot in front and behind our new suburban house. In those early days, it was a teacher, the superintendent of parks in a nearby community, whose inspiring talk motivated my landscaping efforts. Since that time, a few creative words from an enlightened instructor, extension service expert, a garden club lecturer, or talented friend, often leads me to tackle a part of the garden that I've been avoiding.

Nevertheless, throughout the years, it is the written word that generally has the greatest staying power with me. I find the most adhesive advice is in one or another of my favorite books. Let us suppose that under consideration is whether or not to include a new feature in my older garden. In mulling this over, I ask myself again: "What is the basic style of my garden? Will this add-on feature require a change to other parts of the garden that are now entirely satisfactory? How well will the new fit in with the old?" The solution is usually somewhere within the pages of something I have read.

You, too, should answer these questions before committing yourself to an oriental pool, a wildflower meadow, a trough garden, an informal cottage display, or whatever else is on your mind. By extracting a few concepts from the writings of an admired designer, you can decide, at your leisure, whether that new feature will be an exciting addition or an attention-getting misfit.

Oddly enough, when faced with decisions for my naturalistic development, I've returned again and again to read the ideas of Humphrey Repton. This mid 18th, early 19th century Englishman, who invented the term "landscape garden," was one of the first to spell out naturalistic design concepts. Many of them, such as those dealing with unity, utility, convenience, and fitness, are well worth consideration. Repton was able to illustrate his "before and after" plans with maps, diagrams, and water color paintings which he called "red books." They were eventually assembled, bound in red leather, and presented to his clients. Elaborate preparations such as these might have been beneficial to the British on the large estates of that era, but Repton's basic ideas are what truly appeal to me. Many are equally as applicable today when dealing with the smaller spaces of many present day American gardens.

Here are a few of his ideas: rather than rows of the same trees lining a driveway, he liked informal groupings here and there, as though Mother Nature had planted those trees herself. Repton also insisted on making the entire garden a special sanctuary of peace and repose. While such a lofty idea may be impossible in most of our present day city and suburban gardens, somewhere, on every property there is usually at least one space where a private area can be created. And then, too, Repton wanted every aspect of "interference" with art, such as the mechanical necessities of a working fountain or waterfall, to be carefully hidden.

When you, too, have found the workable ideas of a designer that truly capture your attention, then return to his words in moments of impasse. Whether those ideas are oral or written is not important as long as you respond to them. But there are also other ways of jolting our procrastination.

Sometimes, membership in a horticultural society or garden club is the way to go, all the better if it meets regularly in a place that is convenient for you. This is most helpful if your interest is in a particular kind of plant such as rhododendrons, alpines, conifers, perennials, etc. Although there are few, if any, non-professional groups that specialize in landscape planning, garden interests usually overlap, and your club might frequently call upon designers to speak to its members. If not, they need to be encouraged to include them... Often, it is through such an organization that you will be able to meet many like-minded persons, some of them with outstanding properties that you might be able to visit. This can be a truly enriching experience, especially if their garden's soil and climatic conditions are similar to your own.

Don't worry about incorporating the ideas of others into your scheme because your own property and your own interpretations will be unique. How well I remember my first view of a distinctive garden containing outcroppings within a geologically complex ravine. The owner planted it as a series of magnificent rock gardens. The property was eventually deeded to the county and opened to the public. Many years before his death, I asked this gentleman for permission to visit. His answer surprised me: "Yes, but only if you promise not to imitate my ideas." It was amusing to imagine that anyone might try to do so because the site is so unusual. No two properties are exactly the same, and it is highly unlikely that any designer could make a carbon copy of an existing garden.

Throughout our country, public parks, botanical gardens, and arboreta are maintained specifically for both the enjoyment and education of visitors. If you feel intimidated by the size and scope of public developments, there are some organizations that permit visits to private gardens. The Garden Conservancy is such a group. It promotes "Open Days" which are visits to hundreds of home gardener's landscape work on specific days. Very possibly, some of them are in your own area. If you intend to travel further afield, plan your trips to coincide with Conservancy openings. Do remember, though, that if you're looking for applicable ideas, try to locate gardens in the style that suits your garden best. It is interesting to see how divergent our ideas of beauty can be, but suitability to your land should come first and foremost. Formal historic gardens edged with boxwood would be the antithesis of what I am trying to apply to the pastoral environment here at our home.

A walk to observe other landscape designs in your own neighborhood might help you decide what it is that pleases you and what you'd just as soon avoid. Even better, garden travel abroad can be a stimulating experience. But wherever you go, the do-it-yourselfer renovating a garden should not try to compare his own efforts with a grand development employing dozens of professional gardeners. Accept it as a noble work of art worthy of close observation, but leave it—as one would do after admiring a Rembrandt painting—realizing that it is a masterpiece beyond the ability of most of us to acquire.

All in all, if we move out of our own little world for a while, we may find just the right amount of inspiration to stir us into action. But do hurry. Like the butterfly that deserts the flowerless garden, inspiration can quickly fly from our minds. Catch hold of it as soon as you are able and let it awaken your thinking processes.

RECOMMENDED READING

Attracting Birds:

Noble Proctor, "Garden Birds—How To Attract Birds in Your Garden," 1986, Rodale Press

Marcus Schneck, "Garden Bird Facts," 1992, Marboro Books Corporation

Broad-leaved Evergreens:

Brooklyn Botanical Garden, "Handbook on Broad-leaved Evergreens, 1967, BBG

Peter Cox, "Dwarf Rhododendrons," 1973, Macmillan Publishing Co.

Peter Cox, "Guide to Choosing Rhododendrons," 1990, Timber Press

Fred C. Galle, "*Azalea*s," 1987, Timber Press

Richard A. Jaynes, "*Kalmia*—Mountain laurel and Related Species," 1997, Timber Press

Conifers For Landscaping:

Robert Obrizok, "A Garden of Conifers," 1994, Capability Books

P. Den Ouden and B.K. Boom, "Manual of Cultivated Conifers," 1965, Martinus Nijhoff, The Hague

D.M. Van Gelderen and J.R.P. Van Hoey Smith; "The Illustrated Encyclopedia of Conifers," 1996, Timber Press

H.J. Welch, "Dwarf Conifers," 1966, Charles Branford Co.

Designing With Perennials:

Pamela Harper; "Designing With Perennials," 2001, MacMillan Co.

Frederick McGourty, "The Perennial Gardener," 1989, Houghton Mifflin Company

Elisabeth Sheldon; "A Proper Garden," 1989, Stackpole Books

General:

Hortus III, Staff of Cornell University, 1979

Allen Lacy, "The Inviting Garden," 1998, Henry Holt and Company

Allen Lacy, "The Garden in Autumn," 1990, The Atlantic Monthly Press

Patricia Thorpe, "The American Week-end Gardener," 1988, Random House

Donald Wyman, "Wyman's Gardening Encyclopedia," 1986, Macmillan Co.

Groundcover Plants:

David MacKennzie; "Perennial Ground Covers," 1997, Timber Press

Hardscaping:

Gail Damerow, "Fences for Pasture and Garden," 1992, Storey Publishing

Paige Gilchrist, "Making Garden Floors," 2001, Lark Books

Gordon Hayward, "Garden Paths—A New Way to Solve Practical Problems in the Garden," 1998, Houghton Mifflin

Historic Design:

Humphrey Repton, "The Art of Landscape Gardening," 1956, F.W. Dodge Corporation

Landscaping Planning:

Garrett Eckbo, "The Art of Home Landscaping," 1956, F.W. Dodge Corporation

Raymond Korbobo, "Complete Home Landscaping," 1954, Wm. Wise & Co.

A. Paul and Yvonne Rees, "The Garden Design Book," 1988, Salem House Publications

Grant Reed, "Landscape Graphics, 2nd Edition", 2002, Watson-Guphill Publishers

Ann Reilly & Susan Roth, "The Home Landscaper," (architectural styles), Ireland-Gannon Associates, Inc., 1990, Home Planners, Inc., Arizona

Sunset Books Editorial Staff, "Planning and Landscaping Hillside Homes," 1965, Sunset Books

Lawns:

Stuart Franklin, "Building a Healthy Lawn," 1988, Storey Publishing

Turfgrass Resource Center & The Lawn Institute, "Turfgrass Facts" pamphlets, each year

Low-Maintenance:

Erin Hynes and Susan McClure, "Rodale's Low-Maintenance Landscaping," 1994, Rodale Press

Ornamental Shrubs:

Kathleen Fisher, Editor, " Taylor's Guide to Shrubs," 2000, Houghton Mifflin

Roger Phillips and Martyn Rix, "The Random House Book of Shrubs," 1989, Random House

Donald Wyman, "Shrubs and Vines for American Gardens," 1966, MacMillan Co.

Ornamental Trees:

Michael Dirr, "Manual of Woody Landscape Plants," 1998, Stipes

John Fiala, " Ornamental Crabapples," 1994, Timber Press

Frances Tanenbaum, "Taylor's Guide to 50 Best Trees," 1999, Houghton Mifflin

J.D. Vertrees and Peter Gregory, "Japanese Maples," 2001, Timber Press

Donald Wyman, "Trees for American Gardeners," 1965, MacMillan Co.

Ornamental Trees and Shrubs:

Michael Dirr, "Hardy Trees and Shrubs—An Illustrated Encyclopedia," 1997, Timber Press

Perennial Plants:

Allan M. Armitage, "Herbaceous Perennial Plants," 1997; Stipes

R. Phillips and M. Rix; "Perennials," 2002, Firefly Books

P. Harper and F. McGourty; "Perennials, How to Select, Grow, and Enjoy," 1985, HPBooks

Pruning:

George Brown, "The Pruning of Trees, Shrubs, and Conifers," 1996, Timber Press

Lee Reich, "The Pruning Book," 1997, Timber Press

Rock Gardening:

Lincoln Foster, "Rock Gardening," 1968, Timber Press

Baldassare Mineo, "Rock Garden Plants," 1999, Timber Press

George Schenk, "Rock Gardens," 1967, Lane Book Company (California)

John Vivian, "Building Stone Walls," 1979, Storey Publishing

Theme Gardens:

Barbara Damrosh, "Theme Gardens," 1982, Workman Publishing

Weeds, Disease, and Insect Damage:

Peter Loewer, "Solving Weed Problems," 2001, Lyons Press

Barbara Pleasant, "The Gardener's Weed Book," 1996, Storey Publishing

Charles Powell and Richard Lindquest, "Pest and Disease Manual," 1992, Ball Publishing

Michael Smith, Editor, "The Ortho Problem Solver," 1999, or "The Ortho Home
    Gardener's Problem Solver," 2001, Ortho Information Service

George W. West, "A Complete Guide to Pest Control," 1980, Thomson Publications

Window Views:

Heather Angel, "A View From A Window," 1988, Salem House

ACKNOWLEDGEMENTS

Throughout the years, many gardeners in this country and abroad have allowed us to visit, study, and photograph their landscaping. New Jersey's own horticulturally minded folk have been exceedingly helpful in this regard, especially many members of the Watnong Chapter, North American Rock Garden Society. To all of them, I offer my sincere "thank you."

Having a large, exquisite public garden close at hand has also been a plus to my cumulative knowledge of design and plantings. For me, it has been Somerset County's Leonard J. Buck Garden. Since its transition to the county in 1975, its many directors and their staffs have warmly welcomed me and my frequent garden visitors from abroad, and have patiently answered my many design and horticultural questions. I thank each and every one of them.

I also wish to express my appreciation to Landscape Architect Barbara Uniacke and Master Gardener Constantine Kallas for their helpful comments after reading sections of this book.

In addition, I recognize my longtime, devoted friend, the talented artist Pat Greenwald, for her constant encouragement of both my writings and landscape efforts. Although she now lives in Florida, it is my hope that Pat is able to find some parts of this book useful even in the subtropics.

Gardening and writing often compete. In that regard, James McCracken III was of enormous help in keeping our garden attractive during the times when my attention was split in two. James also contributed the amusing drawing on the title page of this book. It is for all his efforts on our behalf that I thank him.

Artist Natalia Petrianyk illustrated the chapter headings with her line drawings for this book, and I thank her for taking time off from her busy schedule to add a light touch to the text.

A special thanks to indexer Camilla Crocker for the splendid work she accomplished in providing an index for my book. Her other suggestions, in studying the text, were equally as valuable.

Last but not least, I acknowledge the role that my husband, Martin, has played in every one of my life's endeavors. His keen eyes, sturdy hands, and logical mind have guided my life for over five decades. Furthermore, his vast knowledge of many mechanical and technical subjects has allowed us to purchase and use the equipment needed to maintain a large "do-it-yourself" garden. And it was he who photographed the scenes taken both here and on our many trips together. But most important of all, Martin, more than anyone else, encouraged my writing and the publishing of this book. When the need arises, he is always there for me as my patient teacher. In that regard, a singular miracle occurred. He was able to teach me how to use a computer and word processor!

PHOTO INDEX

All photos, other than those indicated in the descriptions, were taken at Frog Pond Farm.

INDEX